ECONOMICS AND SOCIETY: No. 4

An Introduction to Quantitative Economics

ECONOMICS AND SOCIETY SERIES
General Editor: Professor C. D. Harbury

ECONOMICS AND SOCIETY SERIES

An Introduction to Quantitative Economics

by

BRIAN HAINES
Lecturer in Economics
Polytechnic of Central London

London
GEORGE ALLEN & UNWIN
Boston   Sydney

ISBN 004 330285 8 hardback
    004 330286 6 paperback

Printed in Great Britain
by William Clowes & Sons Limited
London, Beccles and Colchester

Preface

This book arose from the need to design a second-year undergraduate course for 'economics specialists' that would introduce them to the subject of econometrics on the BA (Social Science) Degree (CNAA) operated by the Polytechnic of Central London since September 1974. However, the word 'econometrics' does not appear in the title because the scope of the book is wide enough to cover not only introductory courses in econometrics but also general courses in applied economics.

The book is designed to introduce students to the methods and jargon used in testing theories or hypotheses in economics and to explain some of the difficulties involved in interpreting results. Intended as a relatively painless introduction to the use of econometric techniques in applied studies in economics, it is a complement to second-year courses in micro- and macroeconomic theory. The book should serve the main functions of enabling students to:

1 Read and comprehend economic literature that employs econometric techniques as a method of analysis.
2 Use econometric techniques themselves in simple studies in class exercises and project work.

In order to achieve these aims, most of the formal mathematical and statistical proofs that are usually found in econometric textbooks have been omitted. This is justified on the grounds that such sophistication is unsuitable at this level for second-year students. However, it is hoped that after reading this book students will develop a sufficient interest in econometrics to pursue this field of study in greater depth at a later stage in their degree. Students who may wish to read further into this subject are advised to look, for example, at R. J. Allard, *An Approach to Econometrics* and J. Johnston, *Econometric Methods*.

The basic requirement for comprehending the book is that the student should have successfully completed a first-year undergraduate basic course in mathematics and statistics and an introductory course in micro- and macroeconomic theory. However, it is useful to student and lecturer alike to be more specific than this since the levels of economics, mathematics and statistics taught on first-year courses in universities and polytechnics vary widely throughout the UK. This applies particularly in the case of the last two subjects.

In the case of economic theory the student is expected to have covered the sort of material to be found in R. G. Lipsey, *An Introduction to Positive Economics* or P. A. Samuelson, *Economics*.

In mathematics, the student is assumed to have some familiarity with the kind of material covered in G. C. Archibald and R. G. Lipsey, *An Introduction to a Mathematical Treatment of Economics*, chapters 1–8, or R. Morley, *Mathematics for Modern Economics*, chapters 1–9. This basically consists of the following: functions; graphs; summation sign; inequalities; logarithms; the exponential function; simple linear models; differentiation; maxima and minima.

In statistics, the student is assumed to have some familiarity with the kind of material covered in H. T. Hayslett and P. Murphy, *Statistics Made Simple*, chapters 1–10, or M. R. Spiegel, *Theory and Problems of Statistics*, chapters 1–14. This basically consists of the following: averages and measures of dispersion; elementary probability; the normal distribution; correlation and regression; tests of hypotheses and confidence limits. (All these topics are revised in chapter 2 of this book.)

The book is arranged as follows. Chapter 1 is an introduction to the uses of econometrics and the general form of an equation involving economic variables. Chapter 2 covers the statistical terminology used in the book; some concepts are revised and some new ones introduced. Chapter 3 explains the method of least squares and simple regression formulae with reference to a worked example. Chapter 4 considers nonlinear relationships, multiple regression and the problem of multicollinearity. Chapter 5 considers the implications of the standard assumptions being invalid, the ways of testing for these violations, and attempts made to overcome the problems that arise. Chapter 6 looks at types and sources of statistical data, the use of lags and dummy variables. Chapter 7 introduces students to several applied studies in macroeconomics that they will be able to relate to their macroeconomic theory course. Finally, chapter 8 considers the use of structural equations and the idea of two-stage least squares.

Exercises for students to work out and/or discuss in seminars are included. In cases where it would be helpful for students to work through an example before reading on, an exercise is included at an appropriate stage within, rather than at the end of, a chapter. Answers to the numerical parts of questions are provided at the end of the book.

I should like to thank David Croome (Polytechnic of North London) for his initial suggestion about the book, Professor Colin Harbury (The City University) for his many helpful comments and suggestions, and the teaching staff of Queen Mary College (University of London) who taught me economics literally from first principles during the period 1969–73.

BRIAN HAINES

Contents

PART ONE

Chapter 1

Introduction to the Relationship between Variables

ECONOMETRICS

There is at present a rapid growth in the demand for a basic working knowledge of econometric techniques. This is due to a desire to understand and to be able to comment on attempts that have been made to test economic theorems empirically and to forecast future events. For example, the results of applying econometric techniques are used as a basis for considering the efficacy of monetary as opposed to fiscal policy or the merits of cost-push as opposed to demand-pull theories of inflation. The use of such techniques is probably the most powerful tool in the hands of an economist since they enable him or her to test the validity of certain ideas or hypotheses when these are applied to real world data.

Econometrics is concerned with both measuring and analysing economic relationships. The meaning of the word 'econometrics' is derived from the Greek words for economy and measure, and it has been suggested that this field of economics has its origins in the fifteenth century (see Schumpeter, 1954). Econometrics has the following uses:

1 *Testing alternative theories in economics.* For example, it may be discovered whether the rate of interest or the rate of increase in output is the more important determinant of investment expenditure.
2 *Providing empirical evidence for use in policy decisions.* For example, the econometrician can estimate the marginal propensity to consume, which provides an estimate of the

simple multiplier; this in turn provides the Chancellor of the Exchequer with a means of estimating the effect that cutting government expenditure by some given amount will have on national income. An alternative example from the field of microeconomics is the estimation of the elasticity of demand for a particular commodity by an econometrician, from which the producer or seller of the good can estimate the effect that a planned increase in price will have on total revenue. A question very near the heart of every commuter on British Rail is: 'Would total revenue actually increase if British Rail were to reduce rather than increase its fares?'

3   *Providing forecasts for economic variables.* For example, short-term macroeconomic forecasting has been carried out at the National Institute of Economic and Social Research (NIESR) for over fifteen years, and their results are published quarterly in the *Economic Review* (see Surrey, 1971). The object of this forecasting model is to predict the major components of GDP – e.g. consumption, investment, exports and imports – from twelve to eighteen months into the future with the aid of econometric techniques. Clearly, the government itself uses forecasts as warning signals to take action via policy changes.

The first stage in econometrics is to formulate an idea or hypothesis into a mathematical model. The second stage consists of collecting the necessary data, which is then analysed by using special statistical techniques. In the third stage the results are analysed and the validity of the model is considered. Econometrics therefore makes use of:

1   *Economic theory*, to give an initial hypothesis.
2   *Mathematical economics*, to present the hypothesis in the form of an equation or number of equations.
3   *Statistical theory*, to suggest the most appropriate method to use for testing the hypothesis.
4   *Data collection*, to test the model.
5   *Decision making*, to decide whether or not to accept the initial hypothesis on the basis of the evidence submitted.

This final stage of interpreting the findings is often the most difficult, because simply discovering that a strong statistical relationship exists between two variables is not a sufficient condition to be able to conclude that one of the variables determines the other. For example, a strong statistical relationship may be discovered between annual changes in GNP and the supply of money in the economy. Does this imply that monetary policy has been highly successful in controlling the economy, or has the government varied the supply of money to maintain a fairly stable ratio between the money supply and GNP? It is very easy to accept an incorrect causal chain of events.

SIMPLE ECONOMIC MODEL

An economic model consists of a set of mathematical equations designed to explain certain economic phenomena, e.g. the quantity demanded and the quantity supplied of some commodity. The simplest form of mathematical equation is a straight line, which has the general format

$$Y = a + bX$$

where Y and X are variables and a and b are constants. If the variable Y is plotted on the vertical axis and the variable X on the horizontal axis, then the constant term a is the intercept of the straight line on the vertical axis (hence telling the value of Y when $X = 0$) and the constant b is equal to the slope of the line (since, by elementary calculus, slope $= dY/dX = b$). An example of an exact linear relationship between two variables is provided by the Fahrenheit and Celsius scales of temperature. If these two measures are denoted by F and C respectively, the relationship between them is that shown diagrammatically in Figure 1.1, or mathematically,

$$F = 32 + \tfrac{9}{5}C$$

Two types of variables can be distinguished: those determined within an economic model are called *endogenous*, whereas variables whose values are determined outside the model are referred to as *exogenous*. The exogenous variables can therefore be taken as given, since they influence the endogenous variables but are themselves determined by factors outside the model.

Alternative names for endogenous and exogenous variables are *dependent* and *independent* variables respectively.

In order to be able to solve a model to obtain unique values for the endogenous variables, a necessary mathematical condition is that the number of equations should be set equal to the number of endogenous variables included in the model. If the model contains more endogenous variables than equations, it will be impossible to solve. If the number of endogenous variables is less than the

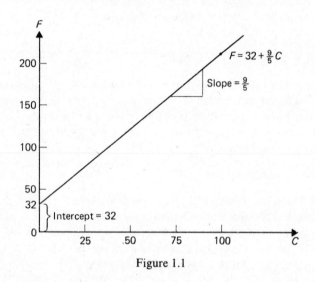

Figure 1.1

number of equations, there will be more than one set of values of the endogenous variables that will simultaneously satisfy all the equations.

Consider, for example, a traditional demand and supply model. Suppose that the market for wheat production includes three endogenous variables: the market price of wheat (P), the quantity supplied during the year (Q_s) and the quantity demanded (Q_d). Since these variables will each be determined within the model at the equilibrium position where quantity demanded equals quantity supplied they are therefore endogenous variables. Let us further suppose that the only exogenous variable in this simple model is annual rainfall (R), which influences quantity supplied, and that the model can be accurately represented by the following three equations:

$$Q_s = -2 + 3P - 0{\cdot}2R \qquad \text{supply equation}$$
$$Q_d = 23 - 2P \qquad \text{demand equation}$$
$$Q_d = Q_s \qquad \text{market clearance equation}$$

In both the demand equation and the supply equation above the effect of a change in price on quantity has been precisely specified and is independent of rainfall. Once a value is assigned to the exogenous variable R (suppose $R = 25$ inches), the above set of equations can be solved to determine the equilibrium values of the endogenous variables price and quantity, i.e. P_e and Q_e at the intersection of the demand and supply curves, where $Q_e = Q_d = Q_s$.

Substituting $R = 25$, $Q_e = Q_d = Q_s$ and $P = P_e$ in the supply and demand equations respectively gives

$$Q_e = -2 + 3P_e - 0{\cdot}2(25) = -7 + 3P_e$$
$$Q_e = 23 - 2P_e$$

Subtracting to eliminate Q_e from the above equations gives

$$-7 + 3P_e = 23 - 2P_e$$

from which

$$5P_e = 30$$
$$P_e = 6$$

Substituting for $P_e = 6$ in the demand equation gives

$$Q_e = 23 - 2(6) = 11$$

Diagrammatically the solution can be presented as shown in Figure 1.2.

ERROR TERM

Although such a simplistic model is a useful starting point in the analysis of a complex situation, it can bear little relation to reality. Many additional factors should clearly be present in both the demand and the supply equations. For example, in the supply equation no account has been taken of the opportunity cost of land used for wheat production; the relative profitability of other

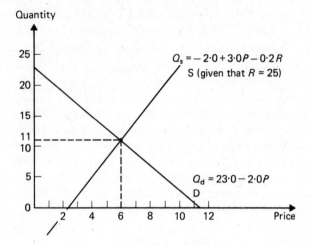

Figure 1.2

crops and foodstuffs will influence the amount of land a farmer will devote to the production of wheat. Moreover, given the amount of land devoted to wheat production the actual harvest will depend upon factors other than just rainfall, e.g. temperature and soil conditions.

Furthermore, in reality the precise form of the relationship between the variables included in the model is not known; for simplicity it was assumed that a linear relationship existed. All that can be said about the supply equation, for example, is that quantity supplied is a function of price and rainfall and that some other factors will also exert an influence. Let us denote the functional relationship by $f(\ )$, which may be linear, quadratic, exponential, etc., and let us denote the influence of any additional factors on Q_s, apart from P and R, by the variable U_1. Therefore the supply equation can generally be expressed as

$$Q_s = f(P, R) + U_1 \qquad (1a)$$

This equation states that price (P) and rainfall (R) are considered to be the most important determinants of quantity supplied, but that the exact mathematical relationship existing between them cannot be specified. It is not possible to collect data on the variable U_1, which takes account of all omitted variables in the supply equation, and consequently it is considered as being unobservable.

Let us suppose it to be likely that the relationship between price, rainfall and quantity supplied is approximately linear. The functional relationship can then be expressed as

$$f(P, R) = a + bP + cR + U_2 \qquad (1b)$$

In this equation a, b and c are constants, referred to as the *parameters* or *coefficients* of the linear relationship. The earlier example, where the supply curve was expressed as

$$Q_s = -2 + 3P - 0·2R$$

involved a linear relationship with $a = -2$, $b = 3$ and $c = -0·2$. The additional variable U_2 included in equation 1b is present because this is only an approximate linear relationship and not necessarily an exact one. The term U_2 therefore represents the extent to which the actual relationship between price, rainfall and quantity supplied differs from the linear form

$$Q_s = a + bP + cR$$

Once again, as in the case of U_1, the variable U_2 is also unobservable since there is no means of collecting data on it.

Combining equations 1a and 1b gives a general supply equation of the form

$$Q_s = a + bP + cR + U_1 + U_2$$

U_1 and U_2 represent the influence of omitted variables and nonlinearity in the supply equation respectively. Since both these are unobservable they cannot be distinguished, and so they are combined and called the *error term* (U):

$$U = U_1 + U_2$$

So the supply equation can be expressed as

$$Q_s = a + bP + cR + U$$

This states that a linear relationship exists between quantity supplied, price and rainfall, and the error term U is also added to take account of the following two elements:

1   *Omitted variables*, i.e. all other variables apart from price and rainfall that may have an effect on quantity supplied.

2　*Effects of nonlinearity*, i.e. the extent to which the true
relationship between quantity supplied, price and rainfall
deviates from the linear form proposed.

STANDARD ASSUMPTIONS ABOUT THE ERROR TERM

The inclusion of an error term in an economic relationship is due
to the fact that economic data, unlike scientific data for example,
is not derived from controlled experiments but from real world
observations that are subject to changes in a large number of
uncontrollable factors. It is therefore impossible to specify exact
mathematical relationships in economics, and so an error term
must be included to take account of random or stochastic
behaviour.

In order to choose an appropriate statistical technique to use
for the purpose of estimating the relationship between economic
variables from a set of data that has been collected, it is necessary
to make certain assumptions about the error term. The simplest
set of assumptions to make is that the error term is an
independently distributed variable with a mean value of zero and
a constant variance. As will be shown in later chapters, any
violation of these assumptions will require an alteration in the
statistical techniques chosen or in the form of the model being
used. This set of standard assumptions made about the error term
can be expressed as follows:

1　The error term has a mean value (or expected value) of zero.
2　The error term has a constant variance over the set of
observations.
3　Each of the set of values of the error term is unrelated to any
other value (or the set of error terms are independent of one
another).

The meaning of these three assumptions will be considered in
greater depth in the following chapter, together with a detailed
explanation of terms such as 'expected value', and 'variance', etc.
The consequences of these assumptions being invalid are covered
fully in chapter 5. However, as a brief illustration consider the
implications if the mean value of the error term is not equal to
zero. Then the estimated values of the parameters in the model

will be biased, which means that they will not be equal to the true value. Corresponding to each observation made on the variables contained in the model there will exist a value of the error term. For example, if a set of 6 monthly observations are taken on quantity supplied, price and rainfall, there will exist a set of 6 values of the error term: U_1, U_2, U_3, U_4, U_5 and U_6. In the general case where n monthly observations are made on the variables, the resulting set of error terms can be expressed, using shorthand notation, as U_t for $t = 1, 2, \ldots, n$. The suffix t is therefore used to denote the time period in which the observations are made (in this case the particular month).

STAGES IN ESTIMATING AN EQUATION

There are two important initial stages that must be considered in order to estimate an equation from a set of data designed to represent a particular economic relationship:

1 *Economic theory has to be used in order to stipulate the range of possible equations that will be feasible.* On the one hand the mathematical form that the relationship between the variables concerned should take must be considered. On the other hand any *a priori* limitations that should be placed on the values of the parameters in the model that will be acceptable also must be considered.

2 *An appropriate statistical method has to be selected and used to estimate the parameters or coefficients in the model.* As previously stated this method will depend upon the validity of the standard assumptions made about the error term. In chapter 3 it will be shown that the method of ordinary least squares is the optimal method to use for estimation provided that these assumptions are valid.

Taking stage 1 above and applying it to our supply equation above, it may be decided *a priori* that the effect of price on quantity supplied is positive and approximately linear, that the effect of rainfall on quantity supplied is negative (beyond a critical minimum level) and approximately linear, and that no other factors have an important effect on quantity supplied. In equation form this is

$$Q_s = a + bP + cR + U$$
$$b > 0 \qquad c < 0$$

where a, b and c are the parameters to be estimated and U is the error term included to take account of omitted variables and deviations from linearity.

Taking stage 2 above, some statistical procedure must then be employed to estimate the parameters a, b and c from the set of data that has been collected on quantity supplied, price and rainfall. A check is then made to ensure that the *a priori* restrictions are satisfied, i.e. that the coefficients of price and rainfall are positive and negative respectively.

Exercise 1.1
1   Explain what is meant by an error term.
2   Why are error terms included in economic relationships?
3   Outline the main uses of econometrics.

Exercise 1.2
Suggest a simple model for each of the following:

1   The demand for and supply of university or polytechnic T-shirts.
2   The demand for and supply of beer.
3   The determination of the level of national income in the economy.

Present the equations you decide to include in your models algebraically and state which are the endogenous and which are the exogenous variables. Also suggest what you consider the main components of any error terms to be. Would you place any *a priori* limitations on the values of the parameters included in your models? Explain your reasons for so doing.

Chapter 2

A Basic Revision
of Statistical Concepts

Before proceeding to consider a suitable statistical method to
adopt for estimating economic models, let us first revise some
basic statistical concepts that will be referred to in the following
chapters.

PROBABILITIES OF SIMPLE EVENTS

Consider tossing a coin or rolling a die. These are examples of
mutually exclusive and *equally likely* events. Outcomes are said to
be mutually exclusive if no two outcomes of an experiment can
occur at the same time; outcomes are said to be equally likely if
no outcome is any more likely to occur than any other.

The so-called *classical* or *equally-likely definition of probability*
states: If an experiment can occur in N equally likely and mutually
exclusive outcomes and if S of these outcomes correspond to the
occurrence of some event A, then the probability that event A will
occur is defined as the ratio S/N. Symbolically this can be
expressed as

$$P(A) = \frac{S}{N} = \frac{\text{favourable outcomes}}{\text{total outcomes}}$$

Hence the probability of getting a head (or a tail) when tossing a
coin is $\frac{1}{2}$ and likewise the probability of getting any of the
numbers 1 to 6 when rolling a die is $\frac{1}{6}$. Clearly probability can
vary from zero (absolute impossibility) to 1 (absolute certainty).

Exercise 2.1
A single card is drawn from an ordinary pack of playing cards. What is the probability that the card is:

(a)   a diamond?
(b)   an ace?
(c)   a seven?

Exercise 2.2
Two dice are tossed. Calculate the probability of obtaining:

(a)   a total score of 6.
(b)   a total score greater than 6.
(c)   a total score less than or equal to 6.

Expected Values, Mean, Variance and Standard Deviation

It is important to distinguish between sample and population. For a sample of n observations on some variable x, i.e. $x_1, x_2, \ldots, x_n$, the sample *mean*, *variance* and *standard deviation* are computed as follows:

$$\text{sample mean} = \bar{x} = \sum_{i=1}^{n} x_i/n$$

$$\text{sample variance} = s^2 = \sum_{i=1}^{n} (x_i - \bar{x})^2/(n - 1)$$

$$\text{sample standard deviation} = s = \sqrt{[\sum_{i=1}^{n} (x_i - \bar{x})^2/(n - 1)]}$$

The above statistics give information about the average value of the sample and also tell the extent to which the sample observations deviate from the mean value.

However, it is useful to have information about the population mean and variance also, and it is in this context that expected values are helpful. A sample is selected from a population. Consider the following example. If a die is tossed 4 times and the scores 5, 6, 2 and 4 are obtained, the sample mean is clearly $17/4 = 4.25$. But if this experiment of tossing a die was repeated an infinite number of times it would be possible to calculate the population mean. Assuming that the die is true, then the probability of obtaining any of the numbers 1 to 6 on any toss of the die is 1/6. Hence the mean value, or *expected value*, from any one toss of the die is obtained as follows, from a weighted sum of every possible outcome multiplied by its respective probability of occurring, i.e.

$$E(x) =$$
$$(1 \times \tfrac{1}{6}) + (2 \times \tfrac{1}{6}) + (3 \times \tfrac{1}{6}) + (4 \times \tfrac{1}{6}) + (5 \times \tfrac{1}{6}) + (6 \times \tfrac{1}{6}) = 3 \cdot 5$$

The term 'expected value' is denoted by $E(\ )$ and is simply equal to the population mean. It is equal to the average value of all possible outcomes if the die is tossed an infinite number of times. The population mean is generally denoted by μ, and therefore

$$\text{population mean} = \mu = E(x)$$

Its main property is as a measure of the central tendency of all the values within a population. Conversely, the population variance is a measure of the spread or dispersion of all of the values about the population mean and is usually denoted by σ^2. Therefore

$$\text{population variance} = \sigma^2 = \text{var}(x)$$

The more concentrated the population values are on the mean the smaller the variance will be, and in the extreme case where all the values are the same the variance will equal zero. Population standard deviation is, of course, the positive square root of population variance.

Four Theorems about Expected Values

The following four theorems apply to expected values:

1   If x and y are two random variables, then the expected value of their sum is equal to the sum of their expected values, i.e.

$$E(x + y) = E(x) + E(y)$$

2   The expected value of a constant is simply equal to that constant. That is, if a is some constant, then

$$E(a) = a$$

3   If x and y are any two random variables and a and b are constants, then

$$E(ax + by) = aE(x) + bE(y)$$

4   If x and y are any two *independent* random variables, then the expected value of their product is equal to the product of their expected values, i.e.

$$E(xy) = E(x) \times E(y)$$

Covariance

Finally, bearing these theorems in mind, consider the concept of covariance between two random variables x and y. Covariance is used to express the degree of dependence that exists between x and y. If the covariance between x and y equals zero, then x and y are uncorrelated or independent of one another. Conversely, if x and y are positively (negatively) correlated or associated with one another, then the covariance between them will be accordingly positive (negative). In terms of expected values the covariance between x and y can be defined as

$$\text{cov}(x, y) = E[x - E(x)][y - E(y)]$$

Expanding this expression term by term yields

$$\text{cov}(x, y) = E(xy) - E(x)E(y)$$

If x and y are independent of one another, then from theorem 4 on expected values,

$$E(xy) = E(x)E(y)$$

Substituting for $E(xy)$ in the above expression yields

$$\text{cov}(x, y) = E(x)E(y) - E(x)E(y) = 0 \qquad (2a)$$

If x and y both have an expected value of zero, i.e. $E(x) = E(y) = 0$, then

$$\text{cov}(x, y) = E(xy) - E(x)E(y) = E(xy) \qquad (2b)$$

Combining equations 2a and 2b gives the condition for *two variables to be independent of one another, given that they both have an expected value of zero*, i.e.

$$E(xy) = 0$$

This manner of writing the condition is frequently encountered in econometric textbooks.

Standard Assumptions about the Error Term

Recall the set of standard assumptions made about the error term as given in chapter 1, which were as follows:

1 The error term has an expected value of zero.
2 The error term has a constant variance.
3 The set of error terms are unrelated to, or independent of, one another.

In the general case where there is a set of n observations on the error term, i.e. U_t for $t = 1, 2, \ldots, n$, this set of standard assumptions can be rewritten thus:

1	$E(U_t) = 0$	Error term has zero mean.
2	$\text{var}(U_t) = \sigma^2$	Its variance equals σ^2 (a constant).
3	$E(U_t U_s) = 0$	For all $t \neq s$. The set of error terms are independent of one another (covariance equals zero).

for all values of $t = 1, 2, \ldots, n$.

This is the conventional format used for expressing the set of standard assumptions.

Exercise 2.3
Table 2.1 gives monthly data on the price charged for beef and the quantity of beef sold by a butcher during one year.
1 Calculate:
  (a) the average price and quantity sold during the year.
  (b) the value of the standard deviation and variance for the two series on price and quantity sold.
2 Plot these observations on a scatter diagram with quantity on the vertical axis and price on the horizontal, and fit a straight-line demand curve by eye through the scatter of points.

Exercise 2.4
If X and Y are two random variables, then the formula for the variance of their sum is expressed thus:

$$\text{var}(X + Y) = \text{var}(X) + \text{var}(Y) + 2\,\text{cov}(X, Y)$$

What does this expression simplify to, if X and Y are *independent* random variables?

Table 2.1

Price per lb (pence)	Quantity sold (lb)	Month
50	130	Jan.
55	130	Feb.
60	115	March
60	125	April
65	110	May
70	80	June
70	105	July
70	90	Aug.
70	100	Sept.
80	90	Oct.
90	70	Nov.
100	55	Dec.

THE SAMPLE CORRELATION COEFFICIENT

The sample correlation coefficient is one of the most powerful tools used in econometrics. It is a number that measures the extent to which there exists a linear relationship between two variables. For a set of n observations on price and quantity, i.e. (p_i, q_i) for $i = 1, 2, \ldots, n$, the sample correlation coefficient is defined by

$$r = \frac{\sum_{i=1}^{n} (p_i - \bar{p})(q_i - \bar{q})}{\sqrt{[\sum_{i=1}^{n} (p_i - \bar{p})^2][\sum_{i=1}^{n} (q_i - \bar{q})^2]}}$$

The value of r must lie within the region $+1$ to -1. If $r = -1$, this indicates a perfect linear relationship between p and q with quantity decreasing as price increases and vice versa. If on the other hand $r = 0$ (or approximately zero), this implies that there exists no linear relationship at all between p and q. A value of $r = +1$ also indicates a perfect linear relationship between p and q, only this time as quantity increases so also does price and vice versa. Clearly then:

1   If $r = -1$, *ceteris paribus* there exists a straight-line demand curve.

2 If $r = +1$, *ceteris paribus* there exists a straight-line supply curve.

3 If $r = 0$, *ceteris paribus* there exists no evidence whatsoever for a linear demand or supply curve.

There are two obvious pitfalls to avoid when interpreting correlation coefficients. Consider a general example where investigation is being made for evidence of a relationship between two variables x and y given a set of observations. First, suppose it is found that a close linear relationship exists between x and y. (The more r deviates from zero in either direction the more pronounced the linear relationship will be, as shown in Figure 2.1.) The

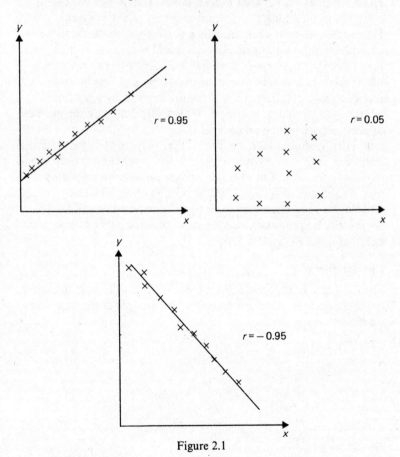

Figure 2.1

correlation coefficient tells nothing about causality. That is, it cannot tell whether variations in x are causing changes in y to occur, or whether variations in x are caused by changes in y, or indeed whether the correlation is spurious. This latter possibility is of course the most worrying from the point of view of interpretation. This problem of causality clearly emphasises the importance of first developing a model based on sound economic theory that specifies the direction of causality and places *a priori* restrictions on the possible values that the parameters can take.

Secondly, it is important to remember that the correlation coefficient is an indicator of the extent to which a linear relationship exists between two variables. It does not indicate the existence of any nonlinear relationship that may be present. Hence, for example, there may be a perfect quadratic, hyperbolic or exponential relationship between x and y, and yet at the same time the correlation coefficient may indicate only a very weak linear relationship. Obviously the importance of first plotting the points on a scatter diagram to look for any sign of a nonlinear relationship should be apparent. Ways of dealing with the problem of nonlinearity will be considered later.

Finally, it should be remembered that r is a *sample* correlation coefficient and as such only applies to the data that has been used in its computation. For example, if data is collected on national income and consumption over a period, say 1945–65, and if a correlation coefficient very close to 1 is computed, it cannot necessarily be presumed that the same positive linear relationship held before 1945 or after 1965.

Computation of r

For the purpose of calculation it is convenient to rewrite the terms in the numerator and denominator of the sample correlation coefficient as follows:

$$\sum_{i=1}^{n} (x_i - \bar{x})(y_i - \bar{y}) = \sum_{i=1}^{n} x_i y_i - n\bar{x}\bar{y}$$

$$\sum_{i=1}^{n} (x_i - \bar{x})^2 = \sum_{i=1}^{n} x_i^2 - n\bar{x}^2$$

$$\sum_{i=1}^{n} (y_i - \bar{y})^2 = \sum_{i=1}^{n} y_i^2 - n\bar{y}^2$$

Therefore the formula for r can be rewritten in the following manner, taking into account the three equations above:

$$r = \frac{\sum_{i=1}^n (x_i - \bar{x})(y_i - \bar{y})}{\sqrt{[\sum_{i=1}^n (x_i - \bar{x})^2][\sum_{i=1}^n (y_i - \bar{y})^2]}}$$

$$= \frac{\sum_{i=1}^n x_i y_i - n\bar{x}\bar{y}}{\sqrt{(\sum_{i=1}^n x_i^2 - n\bar{x}^2)(\sum_{i=1}^n y_i^2 - n\bar{y}^2)}}$$

EXAMPLE

Compute the correlation coefficient from the set of 6 observations on x and y given in Table 2.2.

Table 2.2

x_i	y_i	x_i^2	y_i^2	$x_i y_i$
16	13	256	169	208
12	8	144	64	96
18	15	324	225	270
7	4	49	16	28
12	6	144	36	72
9	10	81	100	90
$\sum_{i=1}^6$ 74	56	998	610	764

Since $n = 6$,

$$\bar{x} = \sum_{i=1}^6 x_i/6 = 74/6 = 12\cdot33$$

$$\bar{y} = \sum_{i=1}^6 y_i/6 = 56/6 = 9\cdot33$$

Thus

$$r = \frac{\sum_{i=1}^n x_i y_i - n\bar{x}\bar{y}}{\sqrt{(\sum_{i=1}^n x_i^2 - n\bar{x}^2)(\sum_{i=1}^n y_i^2 - n\bar{y}^2)}}$$

$$= \frac{764 - (6 \times 12\cdot33 \times 9\cdot33)}{\sqrt{[998 - (6 \times 152)][610 - (6 \times 87)]}}$$

$$= \frac{764 - 691}{\sqrt{(86 \times 88)}} = \frac{73}{\sqrt{7\,568}} = 0\cdot839$$

Exercise 2.5

Use the data in exercise 2.3 on price charged and quantity sold of beef to calculate the sample correlation coefficient. Verify that $r = -0.943$.

THE NORMAL DISTRIBUTION AND THE *t*-DISTRIBUTION

The normal distribution is probably the best-known and most widely used distribution in statistics. In econometrics the assumption is often made that a particular variable is normally distributed. The normal distribution depends upon two parameters: the mean value (μ) and the variance (σ^2). Basically, a

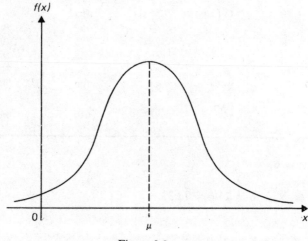

Figure 2.2

probability distribution of some random variable x, often denoted by $f(x)$, enables a calculation to be made of the probability that x takes a certain value or range of values.

The normal distribution is a bell-shaped distribution that is symmetric about its mean value, as shown in Figure 2.2. The equation of the distribution is rather complex:

$$f(x) = \frac{1}{\sigma\sqrt{2\pi}} \times e^{-\frac{1}{2}\left(\frac{x-\mu}{\sigma}\right)^2}$$

In order to compute the probability that x takes a certain range of values, given the mean value (μ) and variance (σ^2) of x, it is necessary to integrate $f(x)$ with respect to x over the range of values concerned. The normal distribution with mean value zero and standard deviation equal to 1 is known as the *standard normal distribution*.

Consider a sample of size n from a normally distributed variable with mean μ, and let us denote the sample mean by $\bar{x}$ and the sample standard deviation by s. Then the random variable

$$t = \frac{\bar{x} - \mu}{s/\sqrt{n}}$$

has a distribution known as a *t-distribution* or 'Student's' t-distribution. The precise shape of this distribution depends upon a parameter known as the *number of degrees of freedom*, which in this case equals $(n - 1)$, or one less than the sample size. The graph of the t-distribution is almost identical to that of the standard normal distribution, i.e. a bell-shaped curve that is symmetrical about zero. As the sample size increases the t-distribution tends towards the standard normal distribution, and in the limit the two become identical.

HYPOTHESIS TESTING AND CONFIDENCE INTERVALS

Suppose a demand curve is to be estimated for some commodity on the basis of data collected on price charged and quantity sold over a specified period of time. The true demand curve is of course a theoretical concept and will thus remain unknown, but it can be written in the following format if it is assumed to be linear:

$$Q_d = a + bP$$

where Q_d = quantity demanded and P = price. The parameters a and b are theoretical quantities whose values are unknown. However, the values of a and b can be estimated on the basis of the data available. Let us denote these estimates of a and b by $\hat{a}$ and $\hat{b}$.

Hypothesis Testing

Hypothesis testing is then concerned with testing hypotheses about the unknown true values of a and b. For instance, it may be wished to test the hypothesis that $b = 0$ against an alternative view that $b \neq 0$. This may be written as:

$H_0: b = 0$ known as the *null hypothesis*

$H_A: b \neq 0$ known as the *alternative hypothesis*

If the null hypothesis is valid in the above example the coefficient of price in the demand equation will be zero, and the implication is clearly that no relationship exists between quantity demanded and price.

Hypothesis testing, however, can never give precise results, since any conclusions arrived at will always be subject to a certain margin of error. Consequently an arbitrary probability is selected, usually 5%, which determines an interval known as the *critical region* or *rejection region*. Then the value of a so-called *test statistic* can be computed, which is known to approximate to a certain distribution, such as a normal distribution or a t-distribution. The critical region is then identified from statistical tables giving the 5% points of the distribution. If the test statistic lies within the critical region the null hypothesis is rejected and the alternative hypothesis is accepted. Conversely, if the test statistic lies outside the critical region, in the so-called *acceptance region*, the null hypothesis is accepted and the alternative hypothesis is rejected.

To illustrate the usefulness of hypothesis testing in economics, consider the example of the coefficient of price (b) in the demand equation, where

$H_0: b = 0$ null hypothesis

$H_A: b \neq 0$ alternative hypothesis

A test statistic equal to $\hat{b}$ (our estimate of b) is computed, then divided by the estimated standard deviation of $\hat{b}$. Denoting this ratio by t, i.e.

$$t = \hat{b}/\text{est SD}(\hat{b})$$

it can be shown that, under the assumption that the error term in the demand equation is a normally distributed variable, this test statistic will have a 'Student's' t-distribution. As indicated earlier the precise shape of the t-distribution depends upon the number of degrees of freedom. Using tables on the percentage points of the *t*-distribution gives the result that with, for example, 20 degrees of freedom there is a 5% probability that the absolute value of *t* is greater than or equal to 2·09.

Therefore the probability of obtaining a value of *t* greater than or equal to 2·09 or less than or equal to −2·09 if the true value of *b* is zero is equal to 0·05. So if such a value of *t* is obtained, the null hypothesis is rejected at the so-called 5% level of significance (which simply means at the 5% probability of wrongly rejecting the null hypothesis).

Figure 2.3 shows the situation diagrammatically. The critical region or rejection region consists of the two tails of the

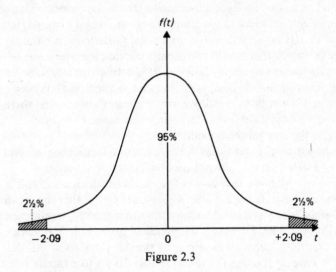

Figure 2.3

distribution to the left of −2·09 and to the right of +2·09. The remaining central area is the acceptance region, so that if a value of *t* is obtained that lies between −2·09 and +2·09, the null hypothesis is accepted at the 5% level of significance. 95% of the distribution lies within the acceptance region, while the remaining 5% of the distribution is divided equally between the tails of the critical region. Thus

$$\Pr\{t \geqslant 2\text{·}09\} = 0\text{·}025$$
$$\Pr\{t \leqslant -2\text{·}09\} = 0\text{·}025$$
$$\Pr\{-2\text{·}09 < t < 2\text{·}09\} = 0\text{·}950$$

which means that the probability that $t \geqslant 2\cdot09$ is equal to $0\cdot025$, etc.

This example has used a two-tail test. One-tail tests also exist, which are used when dealing with alternative hypotheses of the form $b > 0$ or $b < 0$. In such cases all of the critical region lies within one tail only of the distribution.

Confidence Intervals

Confidence intervals follow on directly from hypothesis testing and are a useful asset in econometrics. In our last example the method of testing an hypothesis about the unknown true value of b, the price coefficient in a demand equation, was illustrated. It would clearly be very useful to go a stage further and produce a range of values that would confidently contain the true value of b. Econometricians normally look for 95% confidence intervals for coefficients such as b. Once such a confidence interval has been calculated it can be said that we are 95% confident (or that there is a probability of $0\cdot95$) that this particular range of values contains the true unknown value of b.

It should be apparent that the concept of a confidence interval is very much linked to the notion of variance or standard deviation, which is a measure of the extent to which a variable is dispersed about its mean value. One would expect that the greater the variance or standard deviation the wider the 95% confidence interval would be. However, the practical problem is that since b is an unknown quantity so also is its standard deviation. All that can be done on the basis of the available data is to estimate b (by $\hat{b}$) and to estimate the standard deviation of this estimate. Let us denote this by est $SD(\hat{b})$. As will be shown later, $\hat{b}$ and the est $SD(\hat{b})$ determine the range of the confidence interval for b.

For about 60 observations the range of values

$$\hat{b} \pm [2 \times \text{est } SD(\hat{b})]$$

gives an approximate 95% confidence interval for b. Clearly the width of the confidence interval depends directly upon the estimated standard deviation of $\hat{b}$.

Finally, as an illustration consider the implications of the following confidence intervals obtained for the coefficient of the price variable in some estimated demand equation. (Suppose that

a priori it was expected that a value of *b* approximately equal to
-2 would be obtained.)

(a) $-1\cdot5$ to $-2\cdot4$
(b) $-0\cdot4$ to $-4\cdot1$
(c) $3\cdot0$ to $-7\cdot6$

The 95% confidence interval given by (a) is clearly a good result
that substantiates the initial hypothesis, since we are 95%
confident that the range of values $-1\cdot5$ to $-2\cdot4$ contains the true
value of *b*. The confidence interval given by (b) shows a much
wider range of possible values and makes it difficult to feel
confident about the true value of *b*. However, this result does
indicate that we are 95% confident that the value of *b* is a negative
number within the range $-0\cdot4$ to $-4\cdot1$, which accords with basic
economic theory that a demand curve for any commodity should
have a negative slope. For this reason the confidence intervals
given by both (a) and (b) above are said to imply that the price
coefficient in the demand equation is *significant at the 5%
probability level*.

Now consider the confidence interval given by (c) above. This is
clearly a poor result as can be seen from the wide range of values:
$3\cdot0$ to $-7\cdot6$. In addition, this range contains both positive and
negative numbers so that it is no longer possible to say that the
result accords with basic economic theory at the 95% confidence
level. In any example where a result of this kind is obtained, i.e.
where the 95% confidence interval contains both positive and
negative values, the coefficient is said to be *insignificant at the 5%
probability level*.

PROPERTIES OF ESTIMATORS

Econometrics is concerned with the estimation of parameters, on
the basis of the data available, and with the interpretation of the
results. Estimation is carried out with the help of an *estimator*,
which consists of some formula from which the value of a
population parameter can be guessed, e.g. the coefficient of price
in a demand equation. A specific value of an estimator, obtained
by applying data to the formula, is called an *estimate*.

This section is a review of the three major statistical properties that estimators should ideally possess. For illustration, let us again consider the example of a demand curve where the object is to estimate the price coefficient b.

Unbiasedness

Unbiasedness is the best-known and probably the most important statistical property of an estimator. In terms of expected values it can be said that $\hat{b}$ is an unbiased estimator of b if

$$E(\hat{b}) = b$$

This condition says that if a sufficiently large number of estimates of the unknown parameter b are taken, using the chosen method of estimation, then this method will yield an unbiased estimator if on average it equals the true value b. An unbiased estimator of some population parameter will sometimes give a higher estimate and sometimes a lower estimate than the true value of the parameter. But if an infinite number of estimates were made the mean value of such an estimator would exactly equal the population parameter being estimated.

This property can be illustrated in terms of probability distributions. Suppose that $\hat{b}$, which is an unbiased estimator of b, is a normally distributed variable. Then since it is an unbiased estimator the mean value, or expected value, of the distribution will equal b and the distribution will be as shown in Figure 2.4. This shows that half of all possible estimates are higher and half are lower than the value of the parameter being estimated, i.e. b.

The *bias* in an estimator can be defined as the difference between the mean value or expected value of the estimator and the true value of the parameter being estimated. Hence

$$\text{bias} = E(\hat{b}) - b$$

This is, for any given estimator, a fixed value that may or may not equal zero. If it does equal zero then the estimator will be unbiased since $E(\hat{b}) = b$.

Efficiency

There only exists a generally accepted definition of efficiency, if consideration is restricted to unbiased estimators only. This is a

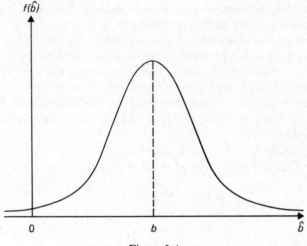

Figure 2.4

reasonable restriction to make since econometricians regard unbiasedness as an essential property of an estimator.

The variance of an estimator is a measure of the dispersion of an estimator about its mean value or expected value. It is clear that if the estimator is unbiased then by definition the mean value of the estimator will be equal to the population parameter being estimated, and therefore the variance is a measure of the dispersion of an estimator around the true value of the parameter being estimated.

A desirable property of an estimator is that this variance or dispersion should be minimised. Consequently an *efficient estimator* $\hat{b}$ of some population parameter b is defined as one that satisfies the following conditions:

1   $\hat{b}$ must be an unbiased estimator of b.
2   $\hat{b}$ must have a smaller variance than any other unbiased estimator of b.

This definition of efficiency therefore rules out any biased estimator, no matter how small its variance may be. Consequently, an efficient estimator is considered to be that unbiased estimator that has minimum variance. An efficient estimator is therefore known as a *best unbiased* estimator, best in the sense of having minimum variance.

Note that an unbiased estimator by itself takes no account of the dispersion of its probability distribution, although the mean value of the distribution will of course be centred on the population parameter being estimated. Hence an efficient estimator takes into account both unbiasedness and dispersion or variance. Consequently, *the pursuit of an efficient estimator is the goal in econometrics*.

Finally, let us briefly consider the notion of *relative efficiency*. Having already stated that an efficient estimator must be an

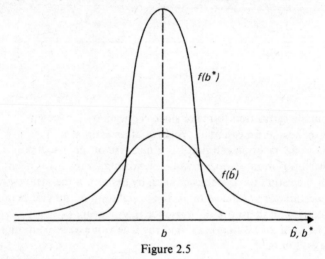

Figure 2.5

unbiased estimator, it is sometimes useful to consider the efficiency of one unbiased estimator of a parameter relative to another. The estimator with smallest variance will clearly be the more efficient estimator of the two. Relative efficiency is measured by the ratio of the variances of the two estimators. For example, if there are two unbiased estimators $\hat{b}$ and b^* of some population parameter b, then b^* will be relatively more efficient if they have the probability distributions shown in Figure 2.5.

Consistency

It has been shown that ideally estimators should be unbiased with minimum possible variance. However, it is sometimes impossible to obtain such estimators even under various assumptions. In such cases the best that can be done is to look for properties that depend on the sample size or *asymptotic properties*.

Therefore an estimator $\hat{b}$ of a population parameter b is defined to be *asymptotically unbiased* if the bias in the estimator tends to zero as the sample size becomes infinitely large. A *consistent estimator* is a logical extension of this, taking into account both asymptotic bias and variance.

A consistent estimator is defined as one for which both the bias and variance approach zero as the sample size approaches infinity. The dispersion of such an estimator around the true value of the parameter being estimated becomes smaller as the sample size increases and in the limit becomes equal to zero. Clearly any consistent estimator must be asymptotically unbiased.

Consistency is important since it gives improved estimates with increasing sample size. It ensures not only that the bias will become smaller but also that the variance or dispersion of the estimates will diminish as the sample data is increased. Hence the probability distribution of the estimator will tend to become more and more concentrated on the population parameter with increases in the sample size.

Chapter 3

The Principle of Ordinary Least Squares and Simple Regression Formulae

METHODS OF ESTIMATION

Consider the estimation of a simple demand model containing just two variables: price and quantity. Suppose, for example, a shopkeeper wishes to investigate the demand function facing him for a particular commodity, and to do this he alters his price (p) every month and observes the effect on quantity sold (q). He considers that price is the only important explanatory variable and that the relationship is approximately linear. So the demand equation can be written as

$$q_t = a + bp_t + U_t$$

where the suffix t denotes the period in which the observations are made (i.e. the particular month), a and b are the unknown parameters to be estimated, and U_t is the unobservable error term.

A method of estimation is required that will give the best possible estimates of a and b. As stated in chapter 2, what is ideally sought is a method that will give efficient estimators of a and b, i.e. minimum-variance unbiased estimators.

Graphical Methods

Let us consider various simple methods of estimation that could be employed. Suppose it is wished to estimate our linear demand curve on the basis of the 6 monthly observations listed in Table 3.1. These observations when plotted yield the scatter diagram shown in Figure 3.1.

Table 3.1

Price (p)	Quantity (q)	Month (t)
10	75	1
7	60	2
30	45	3
20	30	4
40	10	5
50	20	6

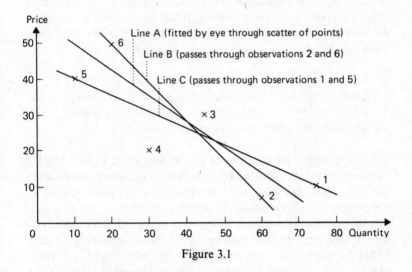

Figure 3.1

Probably the simplest possible way of estimating the demand curve is by eye, as in line A in the diagram. Unfortunately such a method has no advantages except that it is quick and easy to compute. Individual estimates of the parameters a and b would vary according to individual value judgements of which line constituted the best fit in terms of dividing the data evenly above and below the line. And, of course, a person's judgement may be poor, or he might need glasses!

Alternatively, a straight line could be drawn through the points representing the highest and lowest observations on price, i.e. line B passing through the observations for months 2 and 6. Or the observations yielding the highest and lowest values for quantity could be selected and a straight line could be drawn through these, i.e. line C passing through the observations for months 1 and 5. Such methods, however, yield no statistical properties, and since they only take two extreme observations into account they ignore most of the sample information. Obviously no method of estimation can be suitable unless it takes account of all the available data.

The Gauss–Markov Theorem

In chapter 1 it was said that in order to ascertain the relationship between a certain set of variables it is necessary to make certain assumptions about the way in which the error term behaves. The following simplest set of assumptions was introduced:

1   $E(U_t) = 0$ The error term has zero mean.
2   $\text{var}(U_t) = \sigma^2$ Its variance equals σ^2 (a constant).
3   $E(U_t U_s) = 0$ For all $t \neq s$. Its covariance is zero.
for all values of $t = 1, 2, \ldots, n$.

There is a theorem in econometrics known as the Gauss–Markov theorem. This states that under the above set of assumptions about the error term, and a further assumption that the error term is independent of all explanatory variables included in the right hand side of the regression equation, it can be shown that the *ordinary least squares method of estimation* gives best, or minimum-variance, unbiased estimators. The proof of this theorem is highly complex and beyond the scope of this book. The implications of any of the above assumptions being invalid, and the effect on the Gauss–Markov theorem, will be considered in later chapters.

Much of this chapter will consider the method of ordinary least squares (OLS). For illustrative purposes let us take our previous example of 6 monthly observations on price and quantity sold, where it is wished to estimate the linear demand curve:

$$q_t = a + bp_t + U_t$$

where $t = 1, 2, \ldots, 6$. It is conventional to plot the dependent variable, i.e. quantity sold in this example, on the vertical axis of a scatter diagram. The advantages of this convention are that the parameter a can then be interpreted as being the intercept of the true demand curve on the vertical axis (since if $p_t = 0$ then

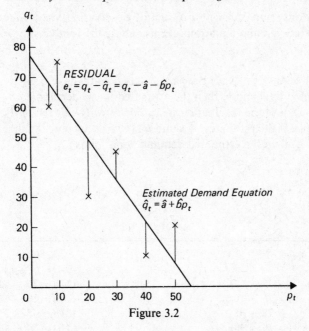

Figure 3.2

$q_t = a$), and that the slope of the demand equation is the parameter b (which is of course constant in the case of a straight-line demand curve).

RESIDUAL TERM

Before proceeding further, let us consider the notion of a residual term. Students often mistakenly identify this with the error term, although the two are quite distinct concepts. The error term is unobservable and measures the difference between (a) each sample observation on quantity sold and (b) the value of q_t that would be obtained from the *true and unknown* linear demand equation:

$$q_t^* = a + bp_t$$

On the other hand, the residual is observable and measures the difference between (a) each sample observation on quantity sold and (b) the value of q_t that can be obtained from the *estimated* linear demand equation:

$$\hat{q}_t = \hat{a} + \hat{b}p_t$$

In Figure 3.2 the residuals are the vertical distances or

deviations from each of our 6 sample observations on q_t to our estimated demand equation. Let us denote the residuals by

$$e_t = q_t - \hat{q}_t$$

for all values of t. Once the parameters a and b have been estimated by $\hat{a}$ and $\hat{b}$, then the estimated linear demand equation is known and the residual terms can be directly calculated. For example, if the estimates of a and b are given by $\hat{a} = 78$ and $\hat{b} = -\frac{3}{2}$, then the estimated demand equation is

$$\hat{q}_t = 78 - \tfrac{3}{2}p_t$$

and the residuals can be computed as shown in Table 3.2.

Table 3.2

$\hat{q}_t \ (= 78 - \tfrac{3}{2}P_t)$	q_t	Residual $e_t \ (= q_t - \hat{q}_t)$
$63.0 \ (= 78 - 15)$	75	$12.0 \ (= 75 - 63)$
$67.5 \ (= 78 - 10.5)$	60	$-7.5 \ (= 60 - 67.5)$
$33.0 \ (= 78 - 45)$	45	$12.0 \ (= 45 - 33)$
$48.0 \ (= 78 - 30)$	30	$-18.0 \ (= 30 - 48)$
$18.0 \ (= 78 - 60)$	10	$-8.0 \ (= 10 - 18)$
$3.0 \ (= 78 - 75)$	20	$17.0 \ (= 20 - 3)$

The error terms, on the other hand, cannot be calculated since the true values of a and b are not known. The distinction between residual and error terms is illustrated in Figure 3.3.

METHOD OF ORDINARY LEAST SQUARES

The ordinary least squares (or OLS) method of estimation is to choose estimators of a and b, i.e. $\hat{a}$ and $\hat{b}$, so that the sum of squared residuals is minimised. This method will give best unbiased estimators of a and b provided that the standard assumptions about the error term are valid.

The reason that the residuals must be squared is to make all the terms positive; otherwise positive and negative values would cancel themselves out when summed together. This is analogous to the formula for variance where deviations from the sample mean are squared.

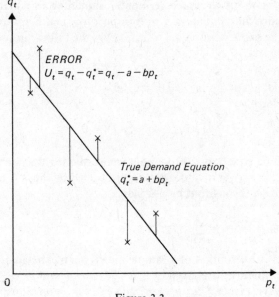

Figure 3.3

Mathematically, if there are n observations on price and quantity the OLS method is to choose $\hat{a}$ and $\hat{b}$ to minimise $\sum_{t=1}^{n} e_t^2$. Let us now derive a general formula for the OLS estimators of a and b.

Our model is

$$q_t = a + bp_t + U_t$$

and the OLS estimators of a and b are denoted by $\hat{a}$ and $\hat{b}$. Therefore the estimated demand equation will be of the form

$$\hat{q}_t = \hat{a} + \hat{b}p_t$$

Let us denote the sum of squared residuals by S, and let us consider the general case of n observations on price and quantity, so that

$$S = \sum_{t=1}^{n} e_t^2 = \sum_{t=1}^{n} (q_t - \hat{q}_t)^2 = \sum_{t=1}^{n} (q_t - \hat{a} - \hat{b}p_t)^2$$

The least squares principle is to choose $\hat{a}$ and $\hat{b}$ so that S is minimised. The necessary conditions for minimising S are that the derivatives of S with respect to $\hat{a}$ and $\hat{b}$ should be set equal to zero. Hence differentiating S with respect to $\hat{a}$ and $\hat{b}$ in turn and setting the expressions equal to zero gives the following two equations:

$$dS/d\hat{a} = -2 \sum_{t=1}^{n} (q_t - \hat{a} - \hat{b}p_t) = 0 \qquad (1)$$

$$dS/d\hat{b} = -2 \sum_{t=1}^{n} [p_t(q_t - \hat{a} - \hat{b}p_t)] = 0 \qquad (2)$$

Summing equation 1 throughout (remembering that summing a constant term over n values gives n multiplied by the constant) and dividing throughout by -2 yields

$$\sum_{t=1}^{n} q_t - n\hat{a} - \hat{b} \sum_{t=1}^{n} p_t = 0 \qquad (3)$$

But from the definition of a sample mean, the mean values of price and quantity are given by $\bar{q} = (\sum_{t=1}^{n} q_t)/n$ and $\bar{p} = (\sum_{t=1}^{n} p_t)/n$ respectively. Hence $\sum_{t=1}^{n} q_t = n\bar{q}$ and $\sum_{t=1}^{n} p_t = n\bar{p}$. Substituting into equation 3 gives

$$n\bar{q} - n\hat{a} - n\hat{b}\bar{p} = 0$$

Therefore

$$\hat{a} = \bar{q} - \hat{b}\bar{p} \qquad (4)$$

Summing throughout equation 2 and again dividing by -2 yields

$$\sum_{t=1}^{n} p_t q_t - \hat{a} \sum_{t=1}^{n} p_t - \hat{b} \sum_{t=1}^{n} p_t^2 = 0$$

Substituting for $\hat{a}$ from equation 4 gives

$$\sum_{t=1}^{n} p_t q_t - n\bar{p}\bar{q} + n\hat{b}\bar{p}^2 - \hat{b} \sum_{t=1}^{n} p_t^2 = 0$$

since $\sum_{t=1}^{n} p_t = n\bar{p}$. Rearranging terms gives the following expression for $\hat{b}$:

$$\hat{b} = \frac{\sum_{t=1}^{n} p_t q_t - n\bar{p}\bar{q}}{\sum_{t=1}^{n} p_t^2 - n\bar{p}^2} \qquad (5)$$

Recall the formula for the computation of the correlation coefficient (r) between two variables x and y as derived in chapter 2. Substituting p and q for x and y respectively, gives the results that

$$\sum_{t=1}^{n} p_t q_t - n\bar{p}\bar{q} = \sum_{t=1}^{n} [(p_t - \bar{p})(q_t - \bar{q})]$$

$$= \text{numerator in formula for } \hat{b}$$

and

$$\sum_{t=1}^{n} p_t^2 - n\bar{p}^2 = \sum_{t=1}^{n} (p_t - \bar{p})^2 = \text{denominator in formula for } \hat{b}$$

Therefore

$$\hat{b} = \frac{\sum_{t=1}^{n} [(p_t - \bar{p})(q_t - \bar{q})]}{\sum_{t=1}^{n} (p_t - \bar{p})^2} \tag{6}$$

Equations 4 and 6 give the least squares formulae for $\hat{a}$ and $\hat{b}$:

$$\hat{b} = \frac{\sum_{t=1}^{n} [(p_t - \bar{p})(q_t - \bar{q})]}{\sum_{t=1}^{n} (p_t - \bar{p})^2} \qquad \hat{a} = \bar{q} - \hat{b}\bar{p}$$

Of course, this result can be generalised to any situation where it is wished to find a linear relationship between any two variables, say x and y. If the model is of the form

$$y_t = a + bx_t + U_t$$

then the OLS estimators will be given by the following formulae:

$$\hat{b} = \frac{\sum_{t=1}^{n} [(x_t - \bar{x})(y_t - \bar{y})]}{\sum_{t=1}^{n} (x_t - \bar{x})^2} \qquad \hat{a} = \bar{y} - \hat{b}\bar{x}$$

EXAMPLE

As an illustration let us derive the OLS estimates of a and b given the data on price charged and quantity sold of beef in exercise 2.3. Suppose we have first calculated the following statistics:

$$\bar{p} = 70 \qquad \sum_{t=1}^{12} (p_t - \bar{p})^2 = 2\,250$$

$$\bar{q} = 100 \qquad \sum_{t=1}^{12} (q_t - \bar{q})^2 = 6\,300$$

$$\sum_{t=1}^{12} [(p_t - \bar{p})(q_t - \bar{q})] = -3\,550$$

The appendix at the end of this chapter contains a more detailed example showing how these expressions can be computed from the original data.

Let us specify *a priori* that $b < 0$, i.e. that the demand curve must have a negative slope. From the OLS formulae,

$$\hat{b} = \frac{\sum_{t=1}^{12} [(p_t - \bar{p})(q_t - \bar{q})]}{\sum_{t=1}^{12} (p_t - \bar{p})^2} = \frac{-3\,550}{2\,250} = -1{\cdot}578$$

$$\hat{a} = \bar{q} - \hat{b}\bar{p} = 100 - (-1{\cdot}578 \times 70) = 210{\cdot}5$$

Hence the estimated demand curve for beef is given by

$$\hat{q}_t = 210{\cdot}5 - 1{\cdot}578p_t$$

The estimated demand curve has an intercept on the quantity axis of 210·5 and a slope of $-1{\cdot}578$. The *a priori* specification that the demand curve should be downward-sloping is met.

VARIANCE OF THE OLS ESTIMATORS

As stated previously, the OLS estimators of a and b will be minimum-variance unbiased provided that the standard assumptions about the error term are valid: namely zero mean, constant variance (σ^2), zero covariance, and the error term independent of all explanatory variables included in the regression equation (i.e. of price in the demand equation example).

Consequently $E(\hat{a}) = a$ and $E(\hat{b}) = b$ under the above assumptions. The formulae for the variances of $\hat{a}$ and $\hat{b}$ are given by

$$\text{var}(\hat{b}) = \frac{\sigma^2}{\sum_{t=1}^{n} (p_t - \bar{p})^2} \tag{7}$$

$$\text{var}(\hat{a}) = \frac{\sigma^2 \sum_{t=1}^{n} p_t^2}{n \sum_{t=1}^{n} (p_t - \bar{p})^2} \tag{8}$$

where σ^2 is the variance of the error term and n is the number of observations made on price (p) and quantity sold (q).

In practice the value of σ^2 is not known since the error term is unobservable. However, the size of the residuals (e_t) is known from the estimated regression line, and these can be used to estimate σ^2. It can be shown that the sum of squared residuals divided by $(n - 2)$ is an unbiased estimator of σ^2. Denoting the estimator of σ^2 by $\hat{\sigma}^2$,

$$\hat{\sigma}^2 = \sum_{t=1}^{n} e_t^2/(n - 2) \tag{9}$$

Now $\hat{\sigma}^2$ can be substituted for σ^2 in equations 7 and 8 to obtain estimated variances of $\hat{a}$ and $\hat{b}$:

$$\text{est var}(\hat{b}) = \frac{\hat{\sigma}^2}{\sum_{t=1}^{n} (p_t - \bar{p})^2} = \frac{\sum_{t=1}^{n} e_t^2}{(n - 2) \sum_{t=1}^{n} (p_t - \bar{p})^2} \tag{10}$$

$$\text{est var}(\hat{a}) = \frac{\hat{\sigma}^2 \sum_{t=1}^{n} p_t^2}{n \sum_{t=1}^{n} (p_t - \bar{p})^2} = \frac{\sum_{t=1}^{n} e_t^2 \times \sum_{t=1}^{n} p_t^2}{n(n - 2) \sum_{t=1}^{n} (p_t - \bar{p})^2} \tag{11}$$

Whereas the true variances of $\hat{a}$ and $\hat{b}$ can never be computed, the formulae in equations 10 and 11 can be used to estimate these variances since they are functions of observed data only. These formulae are extremely useful in econometrics as indicators of the likely degree of accuracy of the estimators $\hat{a}$ and $\hat{b}$.

Estimated standard deviations can of course be found by taking the square root of the estimated variances. Much of the literature in applied econometrics refers to estimated standard errors rather than estimated standard deviations. These two definitions are synonymous.

EXAMPLE

Let us compute the estimated variances of $\hat{a}$ and $\hat{b}$ in our example on the demand curve for beef given 12 monthly observations on price and quantity. First it is necessary to find each of the residuals from our regression equation, square them and sum them together.

$$\sum_{t=1}^{n} e_t^2 = 697{\cdot}41$$

$$\sum_{t=1}^{n} p_t^2 = 61\,050$$

$$\sum_{t=1}^{n} (p_t - \bar{p})^2 = 2\,250$$

Then, since $n = 12$, from equations 10 and 11 respectively

$$\text{est var}(\hat{b}) = \frac{697 \cdot 41}{10 \times 2\,250} = 0 \cdot 031$$

$$\text{est var}(\hat{a}) = \frac{697 \cdot 41 \times 61\,050}{12 \times 10 \times 2\,250} = \frac{42\,576\,880}{270\,000} = 157 \cdot 7$$

Since standard deviation equals the square root of variance,

$$\text{est SD}(\hat{b}) = \sqrt{0 \cdot 031} = 0 \cdot 176$$

$$\text{est SD}(\hat{a}) = \sqrt{157 \cdot 7} = 12 \cdot 56$$

HYPOTHESIS TESTING, CONFIDENCE INTERVALS AND *t*-RATIOS

Let us now consider hypothesis testing, confidence intervals and *t*-ratios and their usefulness in econometrics. If the error term is a normally distributed variable then it can be shown that the OLS estimators $\hat{a}$ and $\hat{b}$ will also have normal distributions and that the ratio of the error in either estimate to its estimated standard deviation (i.e. $(\hat{a} - a)/\text{est SD}(\hat{a})$ and $(\hat{b} - b)/\text{est SD}(\hat{b})$) will have a 'Student's' *t*-distribution. As discussed in the previous chapter, the precise shape of the *t*-distribution depends upon the number of *degrees of freedom*, which is equal to the number of observations minus the number of parameters estimated in the regression line. In estimating two parameters, i.e. a and b, there are $(n - 2)$ degrees of freedom for simple regression, where n is the number of observations.

Use of *t*-ratios

Let us derive hypothesis tests and confidence intervals for b. Econometricians are usually more interested in the coefficient of an explanatory variable (b) than in the constant term (a). The test statistic t, where

$$t = (\hat{b} - b)/\text{est SD}(\hat{b})$$

has a *t*-distribution. In our demand equation example it is wished to test for the existence of a relationship between price and quantity sold. If $b = 0$ then no relation would exist between price and quantity in respect of the true demand equation.

Consider the following hypothesis test:

$H_0: b = 0$ null hypothesis

$H_A: b \neq 0$ alternative hypothesis

With, say, 60 degrees of freedom from tables on the t-distribution, the probability that $-2 < t < 2$ is equal to 0.95. To test the null hypothesis against the alternative hypothesis, the value of the test statistic t is calculated on the assumption that $b = 0$. Thus

$$t = \hat{b}/\text{est SD}(\hat{b})$$

The 5% critical region for the test will therefore be the two tails of the t-distribution given by $t \geqslant 2$ and $t \leqslant -2$. The probability of obtaining an absolute value of t greater than 2 (i.e. $|t| > 2$) if the true value of b is zero is less than 0.05. So if such a value of t is obtained the null hypothesis is rejected and the alternative hypothesis is accepted instead at the 5% level of significance.

Thus if the absolute value of t is greater than 2, i.e.

$$|t| = |\hat{b}/\text{est SD}(\hat{b})| > 2$$

the view that a relationship exists between price and quantity is accepted and any suggestion to the contrary is rejected at the 5% probability of being wrong.

This test is easy to perform and remember, since t is the ratio of the estimated coefficient of b (i.e. $\hat{b}$) to its estimated standard deviation (i.e. est SD($\hat{b}$)). Consequently this is called the *t-ratio*. Since the absolute value of the t-ratio is wanted, the expression is made positive if it is a negative value. If the t-ratio turns out to be greater than 2 the coefficient b is referred to as being significantly different from zero or *significant* at the 5% probability level. Alternatively, if the absolute value of the t-ratio turns out to be less than 2 the coefficient b is referred to as being *insignificant* at the 5% probability level. Of course, the higher the value of the t-ratio in absolute terms (the absolute value of the t-ratio will be referred to simply as the t-ratio), the more highly significant the coefficient will be and the more remote will be the possibility that it could equal zero.

The above result depends on two crucial assumptions: that the error term is normally distributed, and that there are 60 degrees of freedom or 62 observations. However, the result still holds approximately for any number of observations greater than 10. For example, for 20 degrees of freedom the t-ratio should be greater than 2·09 for significance, and for an infinite number of observations the t-ratio should be greater than 1·96 for significance. So the result is almost invariant to the number of degrees of freedom or observations. The only justification that can be offered for the normality assumption about the error term comes from the *central limit theorem* in statistics, which states that the sum of a large number of independent random variables tends to become a normally distributed variable. Only if the error term is thought to contain a large number of independent random variables will this assumption be valid. Nevertheless, t-ratios are widely used in econometrics and provide a useful test for significance.

EXAMPLE

Let us illustrate this concept using our example of the demand curve for beef. It has been calculated that $\hat{b} = -1\cdot578$ and est $SD(\hat{b}) = 0\cdot176$. Therefore

$$t\text{-ratio} = 1\cdot578/0\cdot176 = 8\cdot966$$

This result indicates that the coefficient of price in our demand equation for beef, which satisfies our *a priori* specification of being a negative number to give a downward-sloping demand curve, is highly significant at the 5% probability level.

Confidence Intervals

An alternative approach to that of the t-ratio is to establish a 95% confidence interval for b. Recall that under the normality assumptions about the error term, the test statistic t, where

$$t = (\hat{b} - b)/\text{est } SD(\hat{b})$$

follows a t-distribution. Using tables on the t-distribution for 60 degrees of freedom gives the result:

$$\Pr\{|t| = |(\hat{b} - b)/\text{est } SD(\hat{b})| \geqslant 2\} = 0\cdot05$$

which means that the probability that $|t| \geqslant 2$ is equal to 0·05. Hence,

$$\Pr\{|t| = |(\hat{b} - b)/\text{est } SD(\hat{b})| < 2\} = 0\cdot95$$

Since by definition $|\hat{b} - b| = |b - \hat{b}|$, this can be written as

$$\Pr\{|b - \hat{b}|/\text{est SD}(\hat{b}) < 2\} = 0.95$$

Hence

$$\Pr\{\hat{b} + [2 \times \text{est SD}(\hat{b})] > b > \hat{b} - [2 \times \text{est SD}(\hat{b})]\} = 0.95$$

This important result means that there is a probability of 0.95 that the range of values

$$\hat{b} \pm [2 \times \text{est SD}(\hat{b})]$$

contains the true value of b. Hence this range of values is called a 95% confidence interval for b.

Analogous to our significance test for a coefficient using a t-ratio, it can be said that if the 95% confidence interval contains both positive and negative values the coefficient is definitely *insignificant* at the 5% probability level. On the other hand, if the 95% confidence interval contains *only* positive values or *only* negative values and if the sign and magnitude of the estimated coefficient satisfies our *a priori* specifications (e.g. that the price coefficient in a demand equation must be negative), then it can be said that the coefficient is *significant* at the 5% probability level. This approach is identical to that of using the t-ratio.

EXAMPLE

With reference to our demand equation for beef, the 95% confidence interval for the true value of the price coefficient b is given by

$$-1.578 \pm (2 \times 0.176) = -1.578 \pm 0.352 = -1.930 \text{ to } -1.226$$

Hence we are 95% confident that the range of values -1.930 to -1.226 contains the true value of b.

The results derived in this chapter for t-ratios, confidence intervals and hypothesis tests have all depended upon the probability distribution of the error term. The assumptions made (i.e. that the error term has zero mean, constant variance and zero covariance and is a normally distributed variable) can never be validated although certain checks can be made, as will be demonstrated in later chapters. For this reason t-ratios, hypothesis testing and confidence intervals should not be taken too seriously in economic analyses, although they do provide useful indicators.

Exercise 3.1

1   Use the data on price and quantity given in Table 3.1 at the beginning of this chapter to estimate the coefficients a and b in the linear demand curve

$$q_t = a + bp_t + U_t$$

by the method of OLS.

2   Calculate the estimated standard deviations of $\hat{a}$ and $\hat{b}$.
3   Compute the t-ratio and 95% confidence interval for b.
4   Comment on the significance of these results.
5   Why is the least squares method of estimation used?

Exercise 3.2

With reference to the formula for the variance of $\hat{b}$ (equation 7), i.e.

$$\text{var}(\hat{b}) = \frac{\sigma^2}{\sum_{t=1}^{n} (p_t - \bar{p})^2} = \frac{\sigma^2}{(n-1)\,\text{var}(p_t)}$$

intuitively justify the fact that the var($\hat{b}$) will:

(a) increase as the variance of the error term (σ^2) increases.
(b) decrease as the number of observations (n) and the var(p_t) increase.

CORRELATION COEFFICIENT

Finally let us consider the use and interpretation of the correlation coefficient in econometrics. The correlation coefficient between two variables p and q from a sample of size n is defined to be

$$r = \frac{\sum_{t=1}^{n} [(p_t - \bar{p})(q_t - \bar{q})]}{\sqrt{[\sum_{t=1}^{n} (p_t - \bar{p})^2 \times \sum_{t=1}^{n} (q_t - \bar{q})^2]}}$$

$$= \frac{\sum_{t=1}^{n} [(p_t - \bar{p})(q_t - \bar{q})]}{(n-1) \times \text{SD}(p_t) \times \text{SD}(q_t)} \tag{12}$$

since by definition

$$\text{SD}(p_t) = \sqrt{[\sum_{t=1}^{n} (p_t - \bar{p})^2/(n-1)]}$$

and similarly

$$SD(q_t) = \sqrt{[\sum_{t=1}^{n} (q_t - \bar{q})^2/(n-1)]}$$

As already explained in chapter 2, r is a measure of the extent to which a linear relationship exists between two variables, and $-1 \leqslant r \leqslant 1$.

From the definition of equation 12 and the formula for $\hat{b}$ given by equation 6, it can be obtained that

$$\hat{b} = \frac{\sum_{t=1}^{n} [(p_t - \bar{p})(q_t - \bar{q})]}{\sum_{t=1}^{n} (p_t - \bar{p})^2}$$

$$= \frac{\sum_{t=1}^{n} [(p_t - \bar{p})(q_t - \bar{q})]}{\sqrt{[\sum_{t=1}^{n} (p_t - \bar{p})^2 \times \sum_{t=1}^{n} (q_t - \bar{q})^2]}} \times \frac{\sqrt{\sum_{t=1}^{n} (q_t - \bar{q})^2}}{\sqrt{\sum_{t=1}^{n} (p_t - \bar{p})^2}}$$

$$= r \times \frac{\sqrt{\sum_{t=1}^{n} (q_t - \bar{q})^2}}{\sqrt{\sum_{t=1}^{n} (p_t - \bar{p})^2}} \tag{13}$$

Hence the value of the least squares estimator of b is directly related to the correlation coefficient (r). Squaring and rearranging equation 13 yields

$$r^2 = \hat{b}^2 \times \frac{\sum_{t=1}^{n} (p_t - \bar{p})^2}{\sum_{t=1}^{n} (q_t - \bar{q})^2}$$

Correlation Coefficient Squared

Our demand model can be written in either of the following forms:

$$q_t = a + bp_t + U_t$$

where a and b are the true unknown parameters and U is the error term, or

$$q_t = \hat{a} + \hat{b}p_t + e_t$$

where $\hat{a}$ and $\hat{b}$ are the OLS estimators of a and b and e is the residual term.

Our estimated linear demand curve is written as

$$\hat{q}_t = \hat{a} + \hat{b}p_t$$

Hence

$$q_t - \hat{q}_t = e_t$$

That is, the residual is the difference between the true value of quantity and the value obtained from the estimated demand curve.

The *total sum of squares* is defined to be $\sum_{t=1}^{n} (q_t - \bar{q})^2$, which is a measure of the total variation in quantity demanded.

The *explained sum of squares* is defined to be $\sum_{t=1}^{n} (\hat{q}_t - \bar{q})^2$, which is a measure of the variation in quantity demanded that can be explained by the estimated demand curve.

Finally, there is the *residual sum of squares*, which is of course

$$\sum_{t=1}^{n} e_t^2 = \sum_{t=1}^{n} (q_t - \hat{q}_t)^2$$

This is a measure of the variation in quantity demanded that is left unexplained by the estimated demand curve.

It follows from the three definitions above that the total sum of squares can be divided into its two component elements: the explained and the residual sums of squares. Mathematically,

$$\sum_{t=1}^{n} (q_t - \bar{q})^2 = \sum_{t=1}^{n} (\hat{q}_t - \bar{q})^2 + \sum_{t=1}^{n} (q_t - \hat{q}_t)^2 \tag{14}$$

Let us make use of these definitions to explain the meaning of the correlation coefficient squared (r^2).

Equation 4 gave the result that the OLS estimator of a is given by

$$\hat{a} = \bar{q} - \hat{b}\bar{p}$$

Substituting for this in the equation for our estimated demand curve yields

$$\hat{q}_t = \hat{a} + \hat{b}p_t = \bar{q} - \hat{b}\bar{p} + \hat{b}p_t$$

Therefore

$$\hat{q}_t - \bar{q} = \hat{b}(p_t - \bar{p})$$

Squaring both sides and summing over n observations gives

$$\sum_{t=1}^{n} (\hat{q}_t - \bar{q})^2 = \hat{b}^2 \sum_{t=1}^{n} (p_t - \bar{p})^2$$

Now dividing throughout by the total sum of squares yields

$$\frac{\sum_{t=1}^{n} (\hat{q}_t - \bar{q})^2}{\sum_{t=1}^{n} (q_t - \bar{q})^2} = \hat{b}^2 \times \frac{\sum_{t=1}^{n} (p_t - \bar{p})^2}{\sum_{t=1}^{n} (q_t - \bar{q})^2} \tag{15}$$

From equation 13 it can be seen that the second term of equation 15 is equal to r^2. Therefore a very important result has been obtained: that the correlation coefficient squared is equal to that proportion of the total sum of squares that can be explained by the estimated demand curve, i.e.

$$r^2 = \frac{\text{explained sum of squares}}{\text{total sum of squares}} = \frac{\sum_{t=1}^{n} (\hat{q}_t - \bar{q})^2}{\sum_{t=1}^{n} (q_t - \bar{q})^2} \tag{16}$$

For example, if $r^2 = 0{\cdot}9$ then 90% of total variation in quantity demanded over the period of observations can be explained in terms of our estimated demand curve. As mentioned in chapter 2, caution is required in interpreting correlation coefficients since correlation does not imply causality. All that can be concluded from a high value of r^2 is that a close linear relationship exists between the two variables concerned.

EXAMPLE

Equation 15 can be used to derive the correlation coefficient squared for our example on the demand curve for beef. It has been calculated already that

$$\hat{b} = -1{\cdot}578$$

$$\sum_{t=1}^{n} (p_t - \bar{p})^2 = 2\,250$$

$$\sum_{t=1}^{n} (q_t - \bar{q})^2 = 6\,300$$

Hence from equation 15

$$r^2 = \frac{\hat{b}^2 \sum_{t=1}^{n} (p_t - \bar{p})^2}{\sum_{t=1}^{n} (q_t - \bar{q})^2} = \frac{2{\cdot}49 \times 2\,250}{6\,300} = 0{\cdot}8893$$

The result is clearly impressive since it suggests that 89% of total variation in quantity demanded can be explained in terms of our estimated demand curve. Hence all but 11% of variation in quantity over the period to which our data applies has been accounted for.

Variance and Correlation Coefficient Squared

Dividing equation 14 throughout by $\sum_{t=1}^{n} (q_t - \bar{q})^2$ yields

$$1 = \frac{\sum_{t=1}^{n} (\hat{q}_t - \bar{q})^2}{\sum_{t=1}^{n} (q_t - \bar{q})^2} + \frac{\sum_{t=1}^{n} (q_t - \hat{q}_t)^2}{\sum_{t=1}^{n} (q_t - \bar{q})^2}$$

$$= r^2 + \frac{\sum_{t=1}^{n} e_t^2}{\sum_{t=1}^{n} (q_t - \bar{q})^2}$$

Hence

$$\frac{\sum_{t=1}^{n} e_t^2}{\sum_{t=1}^{n} (q_t - \bar{q})^2} = 1 - r^2$$

Therefore the residual sum of squares can be expressed as a function of the correlation coefficient squared, i.e.

$$\sum_{t=1}^{n} e_t^2 = (1 - r^2) \sum_{t=1}^{n} (q_t - \bar{q})^2 \tag{17}$$

And recalling the estimate of the variance of the error term given by equation 9, i.e.

$$\hat{\sigma}^2 = \sum_{t=1}^{n} e_t^2 / (n - 2)$$

it follows from equation 17 that

$$\hat{\sigma}^2 = (1 - r^2) \sum_{t=1}^{n} (q_t - \bar{q})^2 / (n - 2) \tag{18}$$

SIMPLE AND MULTIPLE REGRESSION

In this chapter only regression involving two variables, i.e. price and quantity, has been considered. This is referred to as *simple regression*. If additional variables such as income, prices of substitutes and complements, etc. had been included, the case would be one of so-called *multiple regression* and the OLS estimators would be more complex expressions.

Even in the simple two-variable example contained in the appendix to this chapter, where there are only 10 observations, the probability of making a computation error when applying the formulae must be fairly high due to the large number of separate calculations required. Special computer programs have been devised to obtain the OLS estimators and the various other statistics. All the econometrician has to do is to feed in the data and put the program into operation. This eliminates the possibility of computation errors and saves considerably in both time and effort. The usefulness of computers will be fully appreciated in the next chapter, when OLS formulae in the case of multiple regression are considered.

EXAMPLE: SUMMARY OF RESULTS

The results of our example on the demand curve for beef can be summarised and presented in the following format:

$$\hat{q}_t = 210 \cdot 5 - 1 \cdot 578 p_t \qquad\qquad r^2 = 0 \cdot 8893$$
$$(0 \cdot 176)$$

where the estimated standard error is given in brackets. An approximate 95% confidence interval for the price coefficient is given by the range $-1 \cdot 930$ to $-1 \cdot 226$ and the t-ratio for price coefficient = $8 \cdot 966$.

Exercise 3.3

Table 3.3 gives quarterly data on aggregate consumers' expenditure (C) and personal disposable income (Y) at current prices over a period of 3 years in £ thousand million.

Table 3.3

Date (t)		Y_t	C_t
Year 1	Q1	6·0	5·3
	Q2	6·2	5·7
	Q3	6·3	5·8
	Q4	6·5	6·1
Year 2	Q1	6·6	5·7
	Q2	6·6	6·2
	Q3	6·6	6·1
	Q4	6·7	6·3
Year 3	Q1	6·5	5·9
	Q2	6·8	6·3
	Q3	7·0	6·4
	Q4	7·1	6·7

(A)   The following set of calculations have been made:

$$\sum_{t=1}^{12} (Y_t - \bar{Y})^2 = 1\cdot08 \qquad \bar{Y} = 6\cdot57$$

$$\sum_{t=1}^{12} (C_t - \bar{C})^2 = 1\cdot59 \qquad \bar{C} = 6\cdot04$$

$$\sum_{t=1}^{12} (Y_t - \bar{Y})(C_t - \bar{C}) = 1\cdot21$$

(B)   The following set of equations has been estimated using the OLS method of estimation:

(a) $C_t = \hat{a}_1 + \hat{b}_1 Y_t + e_{1t}$
(b) $Y_t = \hat{a}_2 + \hat{b}_2 C_t + e_{2t}$

where

$$\hat{a}_1 = -1\cdot32 \qquad \hat{b}_1 = 1\cdot12 \qquad \sum_{t=1}^{12} e_{1t}^2 = 0\cdot231$$

$$\hat{a}_2 = 1\cdot97 \qquad \hat{b}_2 = 0\cdot76 \qquad \sum_{t=1}^{12} e_{2t}^2 = 0\cdot157$$

1   Check the answers in (A) and the value of the OLS estimates in (B).
2   What information do the estimated equations give about any relationships between C and Y?
3   Calculate the estimated standard deviations of $\hat{b}_1$ and $\hat{b}_2$, their t-ratios, and 95% confidence intervals for b_1 and b_2.
4   Use the formula given in equation 16 to compute the value of the correlation coefficient squared for each of the estimated equations.
5   Comment on the results.

APPENDIX: A SIMPLE REGRESSION ESTIMATION

The following is an example of how to estimate a simple regression equation, using OLS method of estimation, from raw data on two variables. The aim is to estimate the equation

$$y_t = a + bx_t + U_t$$

given the 10 sets of data for x_t and y_t shown in Table 3.4.

Table 3.4

t	x_t	y_t	x_t^2	y_t^2	$x_t y_t$
1	11	-8	121	64	-88
2	17	-2	289	4	-34
3	13	6	169	36	78
4	18	13	324	169	234
5	25	10	625	100	250
6	32	20	1 024	400	640
7	21	12	441	144	252
8	17	8	289	64	136
9	25	9	625	81	225
10	33	26	1 089	676	858
$\sum_{t=1}^{10}$	212	94	4 996	1 738	2 551
mean	$\bar{x} = 21{\cdot}2$	$\bar{y} = 9{\cdot}4$			

From the values in the table

$$\sum_{t=1}^{10} (x_t - \bar{x})^2 = \sum_{t=1}^{10} x_t^2 - n\bar{x}^2 = 4\,996 - (10 \times 21{\cdot}2^2) = 501{\cdot}6$$

$$\sum_{t=1}^{10} (y_t - \bar{y})^2 = \sum_{t=1}^{10} y_t^2 - n\bar{y}^2 = 1\,738 - (10 \times 9{\cdot}4^2) = 854{\cdot}4$$

$$\sum_{t=1}^{10} [(x_t - \bar{x})(y_t - \bar{y})] = \sum_{t=1}^{10} x_t y_t - n\bar{x}\bar{y}$$

$$= 2\,551 - (10 \times 21{\cdot}2 \times 9{\cdot}4) = 558{\cdot}2$$

From equation 6

$$\hat{b} = \frac{\sum_{t=1}^{10} [(x_t - \bar{x})(y_t - \bar{y})]}{\sum_{t=1}^{10} (x_t - \bar{x})^2} = \frac{558{\cdot}2}{501{\cdot}6} = 1{\cdot}113$$

From equation 4

$$\hat{a} = \bar{y} - \hat{b}\bar{x} = 9{\cdot}4 - (1{\cdot}113 \times 21{\cdot}2) = -14{\cdot}2$$

From equation 13

$$r^2 = \hat{b}^2 \times \frac{\sum_{t=1}^{10} (x_t - \bar{x})^2}{\sum_{t=1}^{10} (y_t - \bar{y})^2} = (1{\cdot}113)^2 \times \frac{501{\cdot}6}{854{\cdot}4} = 0{\cdot}727$$

From equation 18

$$\hat{\sigma}^2 = \frac{(1 - r^2)\sum_{t=1}^{10} (y_t - \bar{y})^2}{n - 2} = \frac{(1 - 0{\cdot}727) \times 854{\cdot}4}{10 - 2} = 29{\cdot}16$$

From equation 10

$$\text{est var}(\hat{b}) = \frac{\hat{\sigma}^2}{\sum_{t=1}^{10} (x_t - \bar{x})^2} = \frac{29 \cdot 16}{501 \cdot 6} = 0 \cdot 058$$

Hence

$$\text{est SD}(\hat{b}) = \sqrt{0 \cdot 058} = 0 \cdot 241$$

An approximate 95% confidence interval for b is given by

$$\hat{b} \pm [2 \times \text{est SD}(\hat{b})] = 1 \cdot 113 \pm (2 \times 0 \cdot 241) = 0 \cdot 631 \text{ to } 1 \cdot 595$$

and

$$t\text{-ratio for } b = \frac{\hat{b}}{\text{est SD}(\hat{b})} = \frac{1 \cdot 113}{0 \cdot 241} = 4 \cdot 618$$

These results can be summarised in the following format:

$$\hat{y}_t = -14 \cdot 2 + 1 \cdot 113 x_t \qquad\qquad r^2 = 0 \cdot 727$$
$$(0 \cdot 241)$$

where t-ratio $= 4 \cdot 618$ and an *approximate* 95% confidence interval is given by the range $0 \cdot 631$ to $1 \cdot 595$.

Chapter 4

Nonlinear Relationships and Multiple Regression

The results derived in the previous chapter depended upon the validity of the following set of three assumptions:

1 There existed only one important explanatory variable in the model, i.e. price in the demand model.
2 The relationship was approximately linear in format.
3 The three standard assumptions about the error term were correct, and, in addition, the error term was independent of any explanatory variables included in the model. (Also, the normality assumption about the distribution of the error term was invoked to derive hypothesis tests, confidence intervals and *t*-ratios. However, this assumption was not required to obtain the crucial result that the OLS estimators are minimum-variance unbiased.)

Violations of assumptions 1 and 2 above will be considered in this chapter, and violations of assumption 3 will be dealt with in chapter 5.

EFFECT OF NONLINEARITY

Let us first consider the linearity assumption (2). This is not necessarily a very restrictive assumption since it is possible to modify a model to deal with a nonlinear relationship between, for example, price and quantity in a demand model. Consider the following situations.

Known Nonlinear Relationship

First, consider the case where the form of the nonlinear relationship either is known or can be approximated. Suppose our demand equation can be expressed mathematically as:

$$q_t = a + (b/p_t) + U_t$$

Diagrammatically this would yield a true relationship between price and quantity, of the type shown in Figure 4.1. Note that this

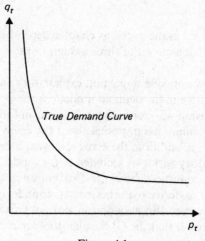

Figure 4.1

equation requires that $b > 0$ to give a downward-sloping demand curve, since it is the *reciprocal* of price that is being considered in this nonlinear relationship.

In this example a new variable can be introduced, i.e. P_t^*, where

$$P_t^* = 1/p_t$$

for all values of t. Therefore the data on price (p) can be transformed into its inverse or reciprocal (P^*), as, for example, in Table 4.1. Then $1/p_t$ can be replaced by P_t^*, for all values of t, in the demand equation to restore our linear demand curve:

$$q_t = a + bP_t^* + U_t$$

Table 4.1

t	Price (p)	$P^* (= 1/p)$
1	10	1/10
2	7	1/7
3	30	1/30
4	20	1/20
5	40	1/40
6	50	1/50

Then q_t is regressed on P_t^* using the OLS method of estimation to obtain estimates of a and b. As mentioned above, $b > 0$ and therefore the relationship between q and P^* will be shown in Figure 4.2.

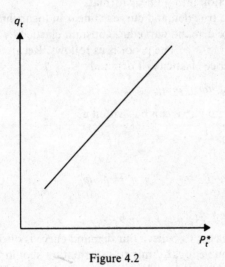

Figure 4.2

Thus if the form of the nonlinearity is known, the data can be transformed to re-create a linear format and then OLS can be applied to the transformed data.

Unknown Nonlinear Relationship

Consider the second more likely case where the form of the nonlinearity is unknown. It is suspected that some relationship exists between two variables, but this relationship cannot be expressed in a precise mathematical formula. This case is clearly more difficult to handle. A common approach is that of a *double logarithmic transformation* of the data. Logarithms to the base e of both sets of data on price (p) and quantity (q) are taken, and then an OLS regression of $\log q_t$ on $\log p_t$ is performed. To see how this works, suppose the true demand curve can be written in the following mathematical format:

$$\log q_t = \log a + b \log p_t$$

This is identical to the nonlinear function

$$q_t = ap_t^b$$

Hence a double logarithmic transformation can transform a nonlinear function into a linear format.

Indeed if the true demand curve is linear in logarithms, as above, then the demand curve has constant elasticity with the elasticity equal to $-b$. The proof is as follows. Recall the definition of price elasticity of demand:

$$e_D = -(dq_t/dp_t)(p_t/q_t)$$

Our true demand curve can be written as

$$q_t = ap_t^b$$

Therefore

$$dq_t/dp_t = abp_t^{b-1} \qquad p_t/q_t = p_t/ap_t^b$$

Hence

$$e_D = -abp_t^{b-1}(p_t/ap_t^b) = -b$$

If there is reason to believe our demand curve is of constant elasticity, a double logarithmic transformation should therefore be applied to the data then $\log q_t$ regressed on $\log p_t$. The OLS estimate of b, the coefficient of $\log p_t$, will enable an estimate of the price elasticity of demand to be made, i.e.

$$\hat{e}_D = -\hat{b}$$

Of course, if $b = -1$ then the demand curve has unit elasticity throughout its entire range, which can be expressed mathematically by

$$q_t = ap_t^{-1} = a/p_t$$

The double logarithmic transformation is often used in econometrics because of the constant-elasticity property and the fact that the application of the least squares method of estimation to the logarithms of the variables yields a direct estimate of that elasticity.

A problem arises when an error term is introduced into this kind of model. In order to get an additive error term in the logarithmically transformed equation, a multiplicative error term is required in the untransformed equation, i.e.

$$q_t = ap_t^b U_t$$

so that taking logarithms gives

$$\log q_t = \log a + b \log p_t + \log U_t$$

This gives a linear relation between $\log q_t$ and $\log p_t$ with an additive error term $\log U_t$. Provided the standard assumptions are valid for $\log U_t$, the least squares regression of $\log q_t$ on $\log p_t$ will yield best unbiased estimators of $\log a$ and b.

EFFECT OF MORE THAN ONE EXPLANATORY VARIABLE

Let us now consider violations of assumption 1 and look at the estimation of multiple regression models with more than one included explanatory variable. It is clear that an equation with only two variables (ignoring the error term) must constitute a very naive and simplistic economic model.

The reasons for including additional explanatory variables into a regression equation are:

1 To obtain a fuller explanation of the economic relationship being analysed.
2 To consider the role that a particular variable plays in the relationship.
3 Because it is suspected that the effects of variation in a previously omitted variable are being incorrectly ascribed to the included explanatory variable. Hence this other variable is introduced into the regression equation to examine its impact explicitly.

4   Because introducing explanatory variables into the equation and removing their effects from the error term (which contains the effect of all omitted variables from the model) reduces the variance of the error term and so *ceteris paribus* reduces the variance of the estimated parameters.

Multiple Regression Model

A general multiple regression model with k explanatory variables is expressed in the following linear equation:

$$y_t = b_0 + b_1 x_{1t} + b_2 x_{2t} + \cdots + b_k x_{kt} + U_t$$

where y_i and x_i ($i = 1, 2, \ldots, k$) are observed variables, U is the unobserved error term, the suffix t indicates the time period, and each b_i ($i = 0, 1, \ldots, k$) is an unknown parameter to be estimated. Although the problems raised are similar to those of the general model above, I shall concentrate on the simplest multiple regression model with just three variables included ($k = 2$), i.e.

$$y_t = b_0 + b_1 x_{1t} + b_2 x_{2t} + U_t$$

Let us again consider a demand model as a specific example and include income (Y) as well as price (p) as explanatory variables. Assuming the model to be approximately linear in format,

$$q_t = a + bp_t + cY_t + U_t \tag{1}$$

Provided that all the standard assumptions about the error term are valid, least squares method of estimation will give efficient estimators of the coefficients a, b and c.

The coefficient b measures the change in quantity demanded (q_t) resulting from a unit change in price (p_t) *with income* (Y_t) *held constant*. Similarly, the coefficient c measures the change in q_t resulting from a unit change in Y_t *with p_t held constant*.

The estimated regression line is

$$\hat{q}_t = \hat{a} + \hat{b}p_t + \hat{c}Y_t$$

where under the OLS method of estimation $\hat{a}$, $\hat{b}$ and $\hat{c}$ are chosen such that the sum of squared residuals is minimised, as before. However, in this multiple regression case the residual is given by

$$e_t = q_t - \hat{q}_t = q_t - \hat{a} - \hat{b}p_t - \hat{c}Y_t$$

Hence the sum of squared residuals is expressed as

$$\sum_{t=1}^{n} e_t^2 = \sum_{t=1}^{n} (q_t - \hat{a} - \hat{b}p_t - \hat{c}Y_t)^2$$

The least squares principle is to choose $\hat{a}$, $\hat{b}$ and $\hat{c}$ in such a way as to minimise this expression.

Stepwise Procedure

A useful approach that helps to explain the logic of multiple regression is provided by the so-called stepwise procedure. Consider the practical problem of measuring the effect of a change in p_t on q_t holding Y_t constant, which is what has to be done in order to estimate b. Because the working material is real data, it is not possible actually to hold income (Y) constant while varying price (p) in order to analyse the separate impact of price on quantity. What can be done, however, is to remove from the data on price (p) and quantity (q) any variation that is related to variation in income (Y). This is equivalent to holding income constant, since any remaining variation in price and quantity can be presumed to occur independently of income (or when there is no variation in income).

If price (p) is regressed on income (Y), the variation in price in the estimated linear equation

$$\hat{p}_t = \hat{f}_1 + \hat{g}_1 Y_t$$

where $\hat{f}_1$ and $\hat{g}_1$ are the estimated parameters obtained by the least squares method, is of course linearly related to variation in income. The residuals from this regression, however, denoted by

$$(e_{pY})_t = p_t - \hat{p}_t \tag{2}$$

are linearly unrelated to income (Y). Thus the residuals from the simple regression of p_t on Y_t, i.e. $(e_{pY})_t$, constitute the part of variation in price that occurs independently of variation in income or with income held constant.

Similarly, if a simple regression of quantity (q) on income is performed in order to obtain the estimated equation

$$\hat{q}_t = \hat{f}_2 + \hat{g}_2 Y_t$$

where $\hat{f}_2$ and $\hat{g}_2$ are the estimated parameters, then the residuals obtained from this equation, denoted by

$$(e_{qY})_t = q_t - \hat{q}_t \tag{3}$$

are also linearly unrelated to income (Y). Therefore the residuals from the simple regression of q_t on Y_t, i.e. $(e_{qY})_t$, constitute the part of variation in quantity that occurs independently of variation in income or with income held constant.

The coefficient b on the price variable in our original equation measures the effect of a unit change in price on quantity with income held constant. It follows from this that, if the effects of income (Y) are removed from both quantity and price to leave the two sets of residuals e_{qY} and e_{pY}, then the coefficient b can be estimated by applying least squares formulae to the equation

$$(e_{qY})_t = b(e_{pY})_t + U_{1t} \tag{4}$$

The estimate of b obtained by this two-stage process is identical to the estimate of b that would be obtained by applying least squares formulae directly to the original equation. This is the stepwise procedure.

Multicollinearity

Let us next consider the concept of multicollinearity. The problem of multicollinearity arises in econometrics when two (or more) of the explanatory variables included in a multiple regression equation are closely related to one another. Suppose, for example, that in the demand equation variations in the two explanatory variables price (p) and income (Y) are closely related to one another. In such a case, even though p and Y may together explain variations in quantity demanded (q) quite well, it nevertheless becomes very difficult to disentangle the separate influences of p and Y and hence to determine their relative importance in the combination. This is the problem of multicollinearity.

Strictly speaking, two variables are described as being multi-collinear if there exists an exact linear relationship between them, but in practice multicollinearity is talked of when there is an approximate linear relationship present.

Recalling the stepwise procedure for obtaining an estimate of the price coefficient b by applying least squares to equation 4, i.e.

$$(e_{qY})_t = b(e_{pY})_t + U_{1t}$$

it follows from least squares formulae that the variance of $\hat{b}$ is given by

$$\text{var}(\hat{b}) = \frac{\sigma_1^2}{\sum_{t=1}^{n} [(e_{pY})_t - \bar{e}_{pY}]^2} = \frac{\sigma_1^2}{\sum_{t=1}^{n} (e_{pY})_t^2}$$

since $\bar{e}_{pY} = 0$. That is, the least squares principle fits a straight line through the data such that the sum (and hence the mean value) of the residuals equals zero. Thus the estimated standard error of the estimator $\hat{b}$ can be expressed as

$$\text{est SE}(\hat{b}) = \hat{\sigma}_1 / \sqrt{\sum_{t=1}^{n} (e_{pY})_t^2} \tag{5}$$

Equation 5 can be used to illustrate the effects of multicollinearity on the estimated standard errors of our estimated coefficients. Clearly, as the degree of multicollinearity between p and Y increases, the residuals from the simple regression of p upon Y, i.e. e_{pY}, will become smaller and smaller. The term in the denominator of equation 5 will consequently also become smaller and smaller, resulting in an increase in the estimated standard error of $\hat{b}$. A similar argument can be applied to the coefficient of income (c) in the original equation, since

$$\text{est SE}(\hat{c}) = \hat{\sigma}_2 / \sqrt{\sum_{t=1}^{n} (e_{Yp})_t^2} \tag{6}$$

which is derived by applying OLS formulae to the equation

$$(e_{qp})_t = c(e_{Yp})_t + U_{2t} \tag{7}$$

Hence the estimated standard errors of $\hat{b}$ and $\hat{c}$, in the original equation

$$q_t = a + bp_t + cY_t + U_t$$

become larger the greater the degree of multicollinearity that exists between p and Y. So it becomes increasingly difficult to obtain accurate estimates of b and c. The t-ratios will become smaller, and the 95% confidence intervals wider, for the parameters b and c. The commonsense interpretation of this phenomenon is that due to the close linear relationship that exists between p and Y it becomes very difficult to determine the separate influence of each of these variables in explaining variations in the dependent variable q.

In the limiting case where there is a perfect linear relationship between p and Y, i.e.

$$p_t = f_1 + g_1 Y_t$$

it becomes impossible to obtain estimates of b and c, and the least squares method of estimation completely breaks down. The reason is that there are no residuals from a regression of p on Y or of Y on p in such a case, since all the observations lie on a straight line, and hence in equations 4 and 7

$$(e_{pY})_t = (e_{Yp})_t = 0$$

for all values of t. And under these circumstances the formulae for the estimated standard errors of $\hat{b}$ and $\hat{c}$, as given in equations 5 and 6 respectively, tend to infinity.

Thus the consequences of multicollinearity, where a close linear relationship exists between the explanatory variables, will be relatively high estimated standard errors. A clear indication of the presence of multicollinearity is a situation in which there is a high value for the correlation coefficient squared (indicating that the explanatory variables can together explain movements in the dependent variable very well), while at the same time the estimated standard errors are relatively high and hence t-ratios are small in value (indicating that it is very difficult to separate the effect of one explanatory variable from another in accounting for movements in the dependent variable).

The problems of multicollinearity tend to increase as additional explanatory variables are included in the regression equation. For this reason it is useful to perform several simple regressions of the dependent variable on each of the explanatory variables in turn, in addition to multiple regressions.

Multicollinearity can be particularly troublesome in estimating *lag structures*. For example, the effect of a change in price on quantity demanded in period t may not be completed in that period but may instead be spread out over several periods. A suitable equation might be of the form

$$q_t = a + b_0 p_t + b_1 p_{t-1} + b_2 p_{t-2} + \cdots + U_t$$

There will generally be a great deal of multicollinearity between the lagged explanatory variables p_t, p_{t-1}, p_{t-2}, etc. Consequently the least squares estimates of the coefficients of these variables will have large standard errors and small t-ratios. Some of the problems of lag structures will be dealt with more comprehensively later on in this book.

EXAMPLE

As an illustration consider the following estimated consumption functions using quarterly data, where C = aggregate consumers' expenditure (£ million) and Y = personal disposable income (£ million):

(a) $\hat{c}_t = -308 \cdot 22 + 0 \cdot 97 Y_t$
           (0·04)

(b) $\hat{c}_t = -255 \cdot 21 + 1 \cdot 18 Y_t - 0 \cdot 21 Y_{t-1}$
           (0·17)   (0·16)

(c) $\hat{c}_t = -175 \cdot 40 + 1 \cdot 14 Y_t - 0 \cdot 28 Y_{t-1} + 0 \cdot 08 Y_{t-2}$
           (0·21)   (0·20)   (0·21)

where estimated standard errors are given in brackets. The value of the correlation coefficient squared is 0·96 in all three equations above. The results clearly show that Y_t is the most important explanatory variable by far. However, the t-ratio of the coefficient of Y_t falls from 24·25 in equation (a) to 6·94 in equation (b) and to 5·43 in equation (c). This is attributable to the multicollinearity that exists between Y_t, Y_{t-1} and Y_{t-2}.

EXAMPLE

Consider another example from the field of macroeconomics, i.e. two versions of the modified accelerator theory of investment. Defining $\Delta' X_t$ as a measure of the increase in industrial production in year t, I_t as gross domestic fixed capital formation (£ thousand million), and K_t as end-of-year-t net capital stock at current replacement cost for companies (£ thousand million), consider the following estimated investment functions using annual data:

(a) $I_t = 0 \cdot 6656 + 0 \cdot 0424 \Delta' X_t + 0 \cdot 0610 K_{t-1}$
               (0·0125)   (0·0049)

(b) $I_t = 0.7199 + 0.0290\Delta'X_t + 0.0012\Delta'X_{t-1} - 0.0258\Delta'X_{t-2}$
$\qquad\quad (0.0136) \qquad\quad (0.012) \qquad\qquad (0.0136)$

$\qquad + 0.0631K_{t-1}$
$\qquad\quad (0.0051)$

where estimated standard errors are given in brackets. The correlation coefficient squared increases from 0.9383 in equation (a) to 0.9468 in equation (b), above when the additional explanatory variables $\Delta'X_{t-1}$ and $\Delta'X_{t-2}$ are included in the investment equation. The t-ratio of $\Delta'X_t$ decreases from 3.4 in equation (a) to 2.1 in equation (b). Once again the effect of multicollinearity among the explanatory variables can be seen.

Exercise 4.1

1 How would you estimate the demand equation

$$q_t = a + bp_t + cY_t + U_t$$

if the values of price (p) and income (Y) could be controlled in such a way that one could be held constant while the other was varied?

2 Why is it difficult to obtain reliable estimates of the parameters b and c when multicollinearity exists between price (p) and income (Y)?

3 Explain the stepwise procedure for obtaining estimates of b and c in the above equation.

Complexity of Multiple Regression Formulae and Calculations

Multiple regression formulae applied to the original data are complex and involve a multitude of calculations. If done by hand or pocket calculator therefore they are likely to result in mistakes. Consequently it is preferable to leave multiple regression calculations to computers.

Denoting deviations from the mean value of a variable by a dot placed over the variable, i.e.

$$\dot{q}_t = q_t - \bar{q} \qquad \dot{p}_t = p_t - \bar{p} \qquad \dot{Y}_t = Y_t - \bar{Y}$$

the OLS formulae for $\hat{a}$, $\hat{b}$ and $\hat{c}$ in the multiple regression equation

$$q_t = a + bp_t + cY_t + U_t$$

can be written as

$$\hat{b} = \frac{(\sum_{t=1}^{n} \dot{p}_t \dot{q}_t \times \sum_{t=1}^{n} \dot{Y}_t^2) - (\sum_{t=1}^{n} \dot{p}_t \dot{Y}_t \times \sum_{t=1}^{n} \dot{q}_t \dot{Y}_t)}{(\sum_{t=1}^{n} \dot{p}_t^2 \times \sum_{t=1}^{n} \dot{Y}_t^2) - (\sum_{t=1}^{n} \dot{p}_t \dot{Y}_t \times \sum_{t=1}^{n} \dot{p}_t \dot{Y}_t)}$$

$$\hat{c} = \frac{(\sum_{t=1}^{n} \dot{Y}_t \dot{q}_t \times \sum_{t=1}^{n} \dot{p}_t^2) - (\sum_{t=1}^{n} \dot{p}_t \dot{Y}_t \times \sum_{t=1}^{n} \dot{q}_t \dot{p}_t)}{(\sum_{t=1}^{n} \dot{p}_t^2 \times \sum_{t=1}^{n} \dot{Y}_t^2) - (\sum_{t=1}^{n} \dot{p}_t \dot{Y}_t \times \sum_{t=1}^{n} \dot{p}_t \dot{Y}_t)}$$

$$\hat{a} = \bar{q} - \hat{b}\bar{p} - \hat{c}\bar{Y}$$

It is easy to see why these calculations should be left to computers! The greater the number of explanatory variables included in the regression equation the more complex the OLS formulae become. It is customary to express OLS formulae in such cases in *matrix algebra notation*, since the result for k explanatory variables (where k can take any value) can be expressed by a simple formula involving vectors and matrices.

Hypothesis Testing in Multiple Regression

The properties and results derived in the last chapter for the simple-regression two-variable case still apply in the case of multiple regression. The only difference is the formulae for the OLS estimators and their estimated standard deviations or errors. For instance, t-ratios and confidence intervals can be derived in the same manner as before for each of the parameters. Multiple regression models, however, offer more opportunities for testing hypotheses than simple regression models do. Apart from testing the hypothesis that the coefficient of some explanatory variable is equal to some specific number (usually a value of zero is used) against a two-sided or one-sided alternative hypothesis, there also exists an *F-test*. This is used for dealing with the more extensive null hypothesis that the coefficients of *all* the explanatory variables included in the regression equation equal zero, which is tested against the alternative hypothesis that at least one of the coefficients is different from zero.

Multiple Correlation Coefficient

The OLS estimators will be best unbiased provided that the standard assumptions made about the error term are valid. In the case of multiple regression the correlation coefficient squared can be defined as the ratio of the explained sum of squares to the total sum of squares, as before, and it represents the extent to which variations in the dependent variable can be accounted for by variations in *all* the explanatory variables that have been included in the model. For example, a correlation coefficient squared equal to 0·6 suggests that 60% of total variation in the dependent variable can be accounted for by variation in *all* the explanatory variables included. It is important to note that it applies to all the explanatory variables and not to any one of them individually.

In this case the correlation coefficient squared is referred to as the multiple correlation coefficient, and it is denoted by R^2 to distinguish it from the r^2 used in simple regressions.

Exercise 4.2

1 Given that the two investment functions using the modified accelerator theory presented in the last example (p. 77) have been estimated by OLS method using annual UK data for 1958–70 inclusive, and that the value of the multiple correlation coefficient (R^2) increases from 0·9383 in equation (a) to 0·9468 in equation (b) when the additional explanatory variables are included, form *t*-ratios for the parameters in the model and interpret the results.

2 Which of the explanatory variables appears to be the most important single determinant of investment?

3 Suggest additional variables you consider to be relevant in a model explaining variations in aggregate investment in the UK.

Exercise 4.3

Table 4.2 gives 12 sets of data for *y*, *x* and *z*. The least-squares simple-regression estimates are:

$$\hat{y}_t = -11{\cdot}89 + 3{\cdot}34x_t$$
$$\hat{y}_t = 151{\cdot}20 - 3{\cdot}18z_t$$
$$\hat{x}_t = 49{\cdot}12 - 0{\cdot}97z_t$$
$$\hat{z}_t = 48{\cdot}96 - 0{\cdot}97x_t$$

1 Use the stepwise method to fit the data to the model

$$y_t = a + bx_t + cz_t + U_t$$

to estimate the coefficients *b* and *c*. First obtain the sets of residuals, i.e. $(e_{yx})_t$, $(e_{yz})_t$, $(e_{xz})_t$ and $(e_{zx})_t$ for $t = 1, 2, \ldots, 12$.

Then regress $(e_{yz})_t$ on $(e_{xz})_t$ to obtain an estimate of b. Finally, regress $(e_{yx})_t$ on $(e_{zx})_t$ to obtain an estimate of c. (Note that each of the sets of residuals can be obtained from calculating the vertical distances from each of the observations to the estimated regression line on a scatter diagram.)

Table 4.2

t	y_t	x_t	z_t
1	107	35	15
2	97	31	20
3	65	21	30
4	62	22	28
5	98	32	15
6	80	30	20
7	120	38	12
8	82	28	22
9	58	22	26
10	82	30	18
11	104	36	15
12	96	32	19

2 Use the formula

$$\hat{a} = \bar{y} - \hat{b}\bar{x} - \hat{c}\bar{z}$$

to estimate the constant term a.

PART TWO

Chapter 5

A Breakdown of the Standard Assumptions made about the Error Term

Recall that the least squares method of estimation will yield best unbiased estimators of the parameters of a linear equation provided that the following set of assumptions about the error term are valid:

1   The error term has an expected value of zero.
2   The error term has a constant variance.
3   The error term has zero covariance.
4   The error term is independent of all explanatory variables.

These assumptions may be judged to be invalid either on *a priori* grounds, from a knowledge of factors that generate the error term and the explanatory variables, or on *a posteriori* grounds, from an analysis of the residuals from the regression. The use of both of these methods will be considered during the course of this chapter, in which consideration will be given to some of the reasonable alternative assumptions about the distribution of the error term, the effect of these alternatives on the performance of the OLS estimators, and whether some alternative method of estimation should be employed.

Let us therefore consider the consequences of each of these assumptions in turn being invalid.

EXPECTED VALUE NOT EQUAL TO ZERO

Suppose that the error term does not have an expected value of zero, so that

$$E(U_t) = h$$

where h is some constant not equal to zero. If, for example, $h = 3$, then the effect will be to shift the estimated regression line upwards by 3 units.

Mathematically this can be shown by writing:

$$U_t = h + W_t$$

where W_t is a new error term that obeys all the standard assumptions. In particular

$$E(W_t) = E(U_t - h) = E(U_t) - h = h - h = 0$$

With reference to a simple demand model of the form

$$q_t = a + bp_t + U_t$$

this equation could be rewritten as

$$q_t = a + bp_t + h + W_t = (a + h) + bp_t + W_t$$

Since W_t obeys the standard assumptions about the error term, the least squares estimator of the constant term in the demand equation will be an estimate of $(a + h)$ rather than of a. Consequently a biased estimate of the constant term will be obtained under these circumstances. If h is a positive number the constant term will be biased upwards, and vice versa if h is negative.

The OLS estimator of b, the coefficient of price, will however be unaffected, and as indicated previously econometricians are generally more interested in this parameter than in the constant term. In most cases hypothesis testing and confidence intervals are not applied to the constant term. There is no way of checking whether or not the assumption that $E(U_t) = 0$ is valid from analysis of the residuals, since under the OLS method of estimation the mean value of the residuals is always equal to zero.

The proof of this comes directly from the derivation of the OLS formulae for the estimators of the parameters a and b. Recall from chapter 3 the first of the so-called *normal equations* (for deriving the least squares formulae). This was derived by partially differentiating the sum of squared residuals (S) with respect to $\hat{a}$ and setting the result equal to zero to obtain

$$dS/d\hat{a} = -2 \sum_{t=1}^{n} (q_t - \hat{a} - \hat{b}p_t) = 0 \tag{1}$$

Hence

$$\sum_{t=1}^{n} (q_t - \hat{a} - \hat{b}p_t) = 0$$

But the residual term is given by

$$e_t = q_t - \hat{q}_t = q_t - \hat{a} - \hat{b}p_t$$

Therefore condition 1 above can be rewritten as

$$\sum_{t=1}^{n} e_t = 0$$

(i.e. the sum of the residuals is always equal to zero under the OLS method of estimation). It follows, of course, that the mean value of the residuals must also be equal to zero under the least squares method.

Thus an analysis of the residuals is of no help as a means of testing whether the expected value of the error term equals zero. Since the violation of this assumption does not affect the important property that the OLS estimators of the coefficients of the explanatory variables will still be best unbiased or efficient, the validity of $E(U_t) = 0$ is generally of no concern.

VARIANCE NOT CONSTANT

Suppose that the variance of the probability distribution from which the error terms are drawn varies, so that

$$\text{var}(U_t) \neq \sigma^2$$

a constant. In such a case, observations for which the error term has a large variance will reflect the linear relationship between the observed variables included in the regression equation less closely than those observations for which the error term has a smaller variance.

If the variance of the error term is constant, then the error terms are said to be *homoscedastic*. On the other hand, if their variance is not constant they are called *heteroscedastic* and this case is referred to as the problem of *heteroscedasticity*.

Suppose that *a priori* there is reason to believe that the variance of the error term is likely to increase over time due to the fact that additional explanatory variables are entering the relationship, which are included in the error term as omitted variables. Hence it is suspected that the variance of the error term is greater for more recent data. Heteroscedasticity could be tested for *a posteriori* by using the residuals from the regression as a proxy variable for the unobservable error terms and plotting the residuals over time. If the dispersion of the residuals increased over time then it is highly probable that the error terms are heteroscedastic. A plot like that in Figure 5.1 would be obtained, in which the dispersion and hence variance of the residuals are increasing over the time period.

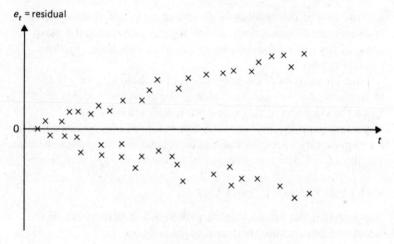

Figure 5.1

The least squares estimators of the parameters will still be unbiased when error terms are heteroscedastic, but better estimates with smaller variance can be obtained by using a *weighted regression*, which gives greater weight or importance to those observations for which the error term has a lower variance. So the OLS method applied to the original data gives unbiased estimators but not efficient estimators of the parameters.

Consider an example of a weighted regression to give unbiased estimators with lower variance. Suppose the heteroscedasticity takes the form:

$$\text{var}(U_t) = dp_t$$

where d is some constant in the simple linear demand model

$$q_t = a + bp_t + U_t \tag{2}$$

In this case the variance of the error term is proportional to the current value of the explanatory variable in any time period t. All the remaining assumptions made about the error term are assumed to be valid, i.e. $E(U_t) = 0$ for all values of t, etc.

Consider multiplying throughout equation 2 by the reciprocal of the positive square root of p_t, to give

$$q_t/\sqrt{p_t} = a(1/\sqrt{p_t}) + b\sqrt{p_t} + (U_t/\sqrt{p_t}) \tag{3}$$

In this transformed equation the new error term is homoscedastic (i.e. has a constant variance), and the expected value of this error term will still be zero since

$$E(U_t/\sqrt{p_t}) = (1/\sqrt{p_t}) \times E(U_t) = 0$$

because $E(U_t) = 0$. And

$$\text{var}(U_t/\sqrt{p_t}) = (1/p_t) \times \text{var}(U_t) = (1/p_t) \times dp_t = d$$

a constant.

Hence if the form of the heteroscedasticity is known or can be approximated, as in the above example, the data can be appropriately transformed so that the new error term in the transformed equation is homoscedastic. To estimate equation 3 above would require a multiple regression of $q_t/\sqrt{p_t}$ on $1/\sqrt{p_t}$ and on $\sqrt{p_t}$ to estimate the parameters a and b using least squares method of estimation.

In this approach, known as a weighted regression, lower weights are being assigned to those observations for which the error term has larger variance, because effectively each of the observations is being divided by the positive square root of p_t, which is proportional to the standard deviation of the error term in period t, since

$$\text{SD}(U_t) = \sqrt{dp_t}$$

This type of approach for dealing with a violation of one of the standard assumptions made about the error term, which consists of first transforming the data in some manner and then applying least squares method of estimation to the transformed data to obtain better estimates with lower variance, is often called a *generalised least squares* approach.

COVARIANCE NOT EQUAL TO ZERO

Suppose that the error terms are no longer independent of one another so that the zero covariance assumption is violated. Mathematically this is

$$E(U_t U_s) \neq 0$$

for $t \neq s$. The error term is generated partially by the effect of omitted variables, and in time series analysis in particular it is

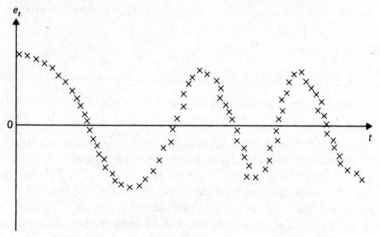

Figure 5.2

often the case that the level of these effects in one period is related to the level in the previous period. This type of behaviour is called *serial correlation* or *autocorrelation*.

A distinction can be made between positive and negative serial correlation. Positive serial correlation implies that if the error term is high in period t then it will also be on the high side in the following period $(t + 1)$. Using the residuals as a proxy variable for the unobservable error terms, Figure 5.2 illustrates a typical positively autocorrelated series.

Alternatively, negative serial correlation implies that if the error term is high in period t then it will be low in value in the following period $(t + 1)$. Again using the residuals as a proxy variable for the error terms, Figure 5.3 illustrates a typical negatively autocorrelated series.

Where serial correlation is present the least squares estimators are still unbiased. However, the estimators will no longer have minimum variance; that is, efficient estimators will not be obtained. In addition, the least squares formulae for the estimated variance and standard errors of the estimators will be biased downwards, so that *t-ratios will be biased upwards and the least squares estimators will appear to be more accurate than they actually are.*

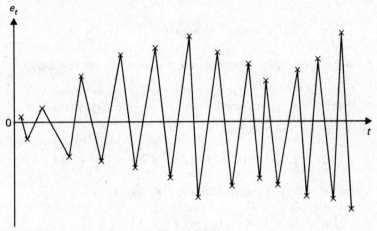

Figure 5.3

Durbin–Watson Statistic

Let us now consider a method of testing for the presence of serial correlation that is both simpler and more accurate than interpreting a scatter diagram of the residuals plotted against time. The Durbin–Watson statistic is commonly used in econometrics to test for the presence of autocorrelation of the error terms, using the set of residuals e_t for $t = 1, 2, \ldots, n$ from the regression equation. This is defined mathematically as

$$DW = \frac{\sum_{t=2}^{n} (e_t - e_{t-1})^2}{\sum_{t=1}^{n} e_t^2}$$

where n is the number of observations.

If there is no serial correlation the DW statistic as defined above will be approximately 2. Alternatively, if there is positive serial correlation the DW statistic will be less than 2, and if there is negative serial correlation the DW statistic will exceed 2. The value of this statistic is constrained to lie within the range 0 to 4.

To prove that $DW = 2$ (approximately) when no serial correlation is present, let us assume that the residuals are independent of one another, i.e. that $E(e_t e_s) = 0$ for all $t \neq s$, with the same variance S^2. It is known that the residuals will by definition have zero mean.

Considering first the term in the numerator of the DW statistic,

$$\sum_{t=2}^{n} (e_t - e_{t-1})^2 = (n-1) \times \text{var}(e_t - e_{t-1})$$

from the formula for sample variance (given that the residuals have zero mean). And

$$\text{var}(e_t - e_{t-1}) = \text{var}(e_t) + \text{var}(e_{t-1}) - 2E(e_t e_{t-1}) = 2S^2$$

since $E(e_t e_{t-1}) = 0$. Hence

$$\sum_{t=1}^{n} (e_t - e_{t-1})^2 = (n-1) \times 2S^2 = 2(n-1)S^2$$

The term in the denominator of the DW statistic is

$$\sum_{t=1}^{n} e_t^2 = (n-1) \times \text{var}(e_t) = (n-1)S^2$$

Therefore

$$DW = \frac{2(n-1)S^2}{(n-1)S^2} = 2$$

If the residuals are independent of one another, i.e. if $E(e_t e_{t-1}) = 0$ for all values of t, the DW statistic will equal 2.

Of course, this result applies to autocorrelation of the residuals and is only a test for autocorrelation of the error terms using the residuals as a proxy variable. Nevertheless any regression equation where the DW statistic is approximately 2 is interpreted as implying that there is little or no evidence of serially correlated error terms. It is customary to calculate and print the value of the DW statistic alongside the estimated regression equation.

Suppose that the residuals are positively autocorrelated so that $E(e_t e_{t-1}) > 0$ for all t. In this case the numerator of the DW statistic becomes $2(n-1)[S^2 - E(e_t e_{t-1})]$, which is less than $2(n-1)S^2$. As the denominator is still equal to $(n-1)S^2$, the DW statistic will be less than 2. The minimum value of the DW statistic is zero, and thus the closer to zero the statistic becomes the greater is the probable degree of positive autocorrelation amongst the error terms.

Alternatively, if the residuals are negatively autocorrelated, i.e. if $E(e_t e_{t-1}) < 0$, then the numerator of the DW statistic becomes greater than $2(n-1)S^2$, and the value of the DW statistic will be greater than 2. The maximum value of the DW statistic is 4, and hence the closer it approaches this value the greater is the probable degree of negative autocorrelation among the error terms.

To summarise, the DW statistic can be interpreted in the following general manner:

$0 < DW < 2$	evidence of positively autocorrelated errors
$DW \approx 2$	no evidence of autocorrelated errors
$2 < DW < 4$	evidence of negatively autocorrelated errors

It should be pointed out that this is a 'rule of thumb' for the interpretation of a given value of the DW statistic. Also, the DW test is for *first-order* serial correlation only and does not cover more complex forms of serial correlation. The DW statistic is in fact a test statistic, and tables exist giving the significance points of it (see, for example, Johnston, 1972, tables A-5a and b, pp. 430–1).

Strictly speaking, all that can be done is to establish upper and lower limits for the significance levels of the DW statistic, which depend upon the number of observations and the number of explanatory variables included in the regression equation. Let us denote these upper and lower limits by d_U and d_L respectively.

EXAMPLE

Let us consider the case where a null hypothesis of no serial correlation is being tested against an alternative hypothesis of positive serial correlation. Using the DW tables at the 5% level of significance gives the result that with, for example, one explanatory variable only included in the regression equation and 20 observations on the variables: $d_U = 1{\cdot}41$ and $d_L = 1{\cdot}20$.

Then the value of the DW statistic is calculated, from the formula involving the residuals from the regression, and the result is interpreted as follows:

1   If $DW < 1·20$ the null hypothesis of no serial correlation is rejected and the alternative hypothesis of positive serial correlation is accepted instead at the 5% level of significance.
2   If $DW > 1·41$ the null hypothesis of no serial correlation is *not* rejected at the 5% level of significance.
3   If $1·20 < DW < 1·41$ the test is *inconclusive* at the 5% level of significance.

First-order Autoregressive Process

Let us now consider a method of partially eliminating the presence of serially correlated error terms. The simplest assumption to make about the form of the autocorrelation is that of the so-called first-order autoregressive process. This is expressed mathematically as

$$U_t = cU_{t-1} + W_t$$

where U_t is the error term in period t in the equation being estimated, c is some constant, and W_t is a new error term that is assumed to obey all the standard assumptions of zero mean, constant variance and no serial correlation. The above model implies that U_t is linearly related to U_{t-1} for all values of t, with no constant term present but with a new error term included to take account of any other effects. The parameter c is unknown.

Suppose the following equation is being estimated:

$$y_t = bx_t + U_t \tag{4}$$

given a first-order autoregressive process for U_t, i.e.

$$U_t = cU_{t-1} + W_t \tag{5}$$

Multiplying throughout equation 4 by $-c$ and lagging one time period gives

$$-cy_{t-1} = -cbx_{t-1} - cU_{t-1} \tag{6}$$

Adding equations 4 and 6 gives

$$y_t - cy_{t-1} = b(x_t - cx_{t-1}) + U_t - cU_{t-1}$$

But from equation 5

$$U_t - cU_{t-1} = W_t$$

and hence

$$y_t - cy_{t-1} = b(x_t - cx_{t-1}) + W_t \tag{7}$$

Since the error term in equation 7 obeys all the standard assumptions about the error term, the application of least squares to the transformed data $(y_t - cy_{t-1})$ and $(x_t - cx_{t-1})$ in equation 7 will give a minimum-variance unbiased estimator of the parameter b. This is the generalised least squares approach, analogous to the weighted regression approach considered earlier for dealing with heteroscedasticity. In both cases the original data is transformed in order to obtain better estimates when the least squares method of estimation is applied.

Estimation of Parameter c

However, the problem with the above procedure is of course that the parameter c is unknown. For simplicity it is often assumed that $c = 1$, so that in equation 7 first differences are taken and $(y_t - y_{t-1})$ is regressed on $(x_t - x_{t-1})$. First differences are generally denoted by the symbol Δ. This is known as the *method of first differences*, designed to reduce the extent of serial correlation. The success of this approach will depend upon the validity of the first-order autoregressive process for generating the error terms and on the assumption that $c = 1$.

A more sophisticated approach is to estimate the value of c from the residuals. Using the residuals as a proxy variable for the unknown error terms and substituting in equation 5 gives

$$e_t = ce_{t-1} + W_t$$

where e_t is the residual in period t. Then least squares formulae can be applied to this equation to estimate c by

$$\hat{c} = \frac{\sum_{t=2}^{n} e_t e_{t-1}}{\sum_{t=2}^{n} e_{t-1}^2}$$

since the mean value of the residuals is zero. Given $\hat{c}$, least squares formulae can then be applied to the transformed data $(y_t - \hat{c}y_{t-1})$ and $(x_t - \hat{c}x_{t-1})$.

In fact c can be estimated directly from the DW statistic. Recall that

$$DW = \frac{\sum_{t=2}^{n} (e_t - e_{t-1})^2}{\sum_{t=1}^{n} e_t^2}$$

$$= \frac{\sum_{t=2}^{n} e_t^2 + \sum_{t=2}^{n} e_{t-1}^2 - 2\sum_{t=2}^{n} e_t e_{t-1}}{\sum_{t=1}^{n} e_t^2}$$

But

$$\sum_{t=2}^{n} e_{t-1}^2 = \sum_{t=1}^{n-1} e_t^2 \quad \text{and} \quad \sum_{t=1}^{n} e_t^2 = \sum_{t=2}^{n+1} e_{t-1}^2$$

Therefore

$$DW = \frac{\sum_{t=2}^{n} e_t^2 + \sum_{t=1}^{n-1} e_t^2}{\sum_{t=1}^{n} e_t^2} - 2 \times \frac{\sum_{t=2}^{n} e_t e_{t-1}}{\sum_{t=2}^{n+1} e_{t-1}^2}$$

$$\approx 2 - 2\hat{c}$$

The DW statistic is thus approximately equal to $2(1 - \hat{c})$. Given the value of the DW statistic, the parameter c can be estimated from the equation

$$DW = 2(1 - \hat{c})$$

Exercise 5.1

1 What rationale can be offered for the first-order autoregressive process for generating error terms, i.e.

$$U_t = cU_{t-1} + W_t$$

where U_t is the value of the error term in period t and W_t is a completely random series?

2 Is it a reasonable process to assume in economic models?

3 How does the length of the observation period (i.e. monthly, quarterly, annually) affect the process?

NOT INDEPENDENT OF ALL EXPLANATORY VARIABLES

Consider as a final violation of the standard assumptions concerning the error term the case where the error term is not independent of all the explanatory variables included in the regression equation. Referring back to our simple linear demand model

$$q_t = a + bp_t + U_t \tag{8}$$

suppose that the omitted variables included in the error term vary in a similar way to price, so that U_t is related to p_t. Suppose further that the error term is proportionately related to price, with a new error term included in the relationship so that

$$U_t = dp_t + W_t \tag{9}$$

where W_t obeys all the standard assumptions.

Substituting equation 9 in equation 8 yields

$$q_t = a + bp_t + dp_t + W_t = a + (b + d)p_t + W_t$$

The least squares estimator of the coefficient of p_t will be an estimate of $(b + d)$ rather than of b. Therefore the estimator of the price coefficient in equation 8 will be biased. If d is some positive number, implying that U_t and p_t are positively correlated, then the least squares estimator of the coefficient of p_t will be biased upwards, and vice versa if d is negative.

Using the residuals as a proxy variable for the unobservable error terms, a test can be made for a possible relationship between the error term and an explanatory variable by analysis of a scatter diagram plotting the residuals against the corresponding values of the explanatory variable.

There are four circumstances in which the error term may be related to an explanatory variable resulting in a biased estimate of the coefficient of this variable, using OLS method of estimation. Each of these circumstances will be considered in turn.

Case 1

Suppose that the omitted variables included in the error term are related to an explanatory variable included in the regression equation, so that the error term will not be independent of this variable. In this case, if the omitted variables are measurable they should be included explicitly in the regression equation to remove their influence from the error term.

Case 2

Suppose that the explanatory variable is an endogenous variable, i.e. one whose value is determined within the model. This is clearly the case in a demand or supply model where the explanatory variable price is endogenous. In such circumstances two or more simultaneous equations are required to complete the model. This case will be considered in greater depth in chapter 8. Suffice to say that if an explanatory variable is endogenous rather than exogenous to the model, then its value will generally be related to the value of the error term and the least squares estimator of its coefficient will be biased. The reason for this and alternative methods of estimation in such cases will be dealt with later.

Case 3

A third case in which the error term will be related to an explanatory variable is a variant of the previous case. If the explanatory variable is a lagged endogenous variable, and if in addition the error terms are autocorrelated, then it can be shown that the error term will not be independent of the variable, resulting in a biased estimate of its coefficient using the OLS method. This particular case will be covered in greater depth in the following chapter.

An example of a lagged endogenous variable is given by p_{t-1} in a supply equation:

$$q_t = a + bp_{t-1} + U_t$$

Quantity supplied in this example depends upon price charged in the previous time period $(t-1)$. Price is an endogenous variable since it is determined within a demand–supply model. Hence price in the previous time period (p_{t-1}) is a lagged endogenous variable.

Case 4

The final case in which the error term will not be independent of an explanatory variable occurs when there is a measurement error in the explanatory variable. Consider a general case where investigation is being made into the relationship between two variables x and y, i.e.

$$y_t = a + bx_t + U_t \tag{10}$$

It is believed that the relationship between the true values of x and y is approximately linear, and the aim is to estimate the coefficients a and b given a set of data on x and y. However, let us suppose that the data contains measurement errors in the explanatory variable x. Therefore instead of the true values of x_t $(t = 1, 2, \ldots, n)$ being observed, values of X_t $(t = 1, 2, \ldots, n)$ are observed, where

$$X_t = x_t + v_t$$

for $t = 1, 2, \ldots, n$ and v_t is the error in measuring the tth value of x. Suppose that v_t is a random variable with zero mean.

Substituting for x_t in the regression equation 10 above gives

$$y_t = a + b(X_t - v_t) + U_t = a + bX_t + (U_t - bv_t)$$

Thus the error term in the observed relationship between y_t and X_t is given by $(U_t - bv_t)$, which contains part of the measurement error v_t on the variable x_t. The error term $(U_t - bv_t)$ is clearly not independent of the observed value of x_t, i.e. X_t. This will bias the estimate of b using the least squares method. The importance of accurate data is evident.

Exercise 5.2
Table 5.1 gives two sets of data on price and quantity supplied of some commodity taken at regular time intervals. The linear supply equation

$$q_t = a + bp_t + U_t$$

has been estimated for each set of data, and the values of $\hat{a}$, $\hat{b}$, est SE($\hat{b}$) and r^2 are given.

1   For each set of observations draw graphs of the estimated supply curves and of the residuals, given by

$$e_t = q_t - \hat{a} - \hat{b}p_t$$

against both p_t and t.

Table 5.1

	Data A		Data B	
t	*p*	*q*	*p*	*q*
1	4	2	5	0·5
2	2	1	13·5	5·5
3	7	9	23	12
4	10	4·5	18·5	9
5	24	15·5	6	3·5
6	3	8	14·5	9·5
7	7·5	2·5	21	12
8	5·5	4·5	8	6
9	4	5	2·5	4
10	2	5	11·5	10
11	5	7	18	14
12	8	6·5	23	19
$\hat{a} =$		2·49	0·21	
$\hat{b} =$		0·50	0·63	
est SE($\hat{b}$) =		0·13	0·11	
$r^2 =$		0·58	0·75	

2   Comment on the apparent validity of the standard assumptions
    made about the error term and on the results obtained for
    each set of data.

Chapter 6

Statistical Data, Distributed Lag Models and Dummy Variables

STATISTICAL DATA

Types of Data

All the results so far developed and the examples considered have been based upon the analysis of *time-series data*. However, econometric principles can also be applied to *cross-section data*. Observations on economic variables that are made over time give time-series data. On the other hand, observations made over individuals, groups of individuals, objects or geographical areas, etc. at a particular moment in time give cross-section data. Hence the subscript t may refer to the tth time period or alternatively to the tth individual, object or geographical area, etc.

Generally, macroeconomic data is time-series data, since it deals with aggregate relationships, and microeconomic data collected on individual households or firms is cross-section data taken from sample surveys.

As an example of the use of cross-section data, consider the findings of an interindustry study by Amey (1964). Amey tested for evidence of a positive correlation between diversification of firms' activities into other industries and their expenditure on research and development. He believed that diversification had been stimulated by a significant increase in research carried out by firms since the last war, leading to a lowering of industrial boundaries and expansion into other industries. Amey tested this hypothesis using UK cross-section data on twenty-five industry groups for 1960. As a measure of diversification he used the ratio of a firm's nonprimary output to its total output. Aggregating over all firms in a particular industry group he obtained a measure of the degree of diversification within that industry expressed in percentage terms. As a measure of research and development in an industry he took figures on the number of qualified scientists and engineers engaged on research and development projects. Defining Y_t as the degree of diversification of firms in the tth industry and X_t as scientific manpower engaged in research projects in the tth industry (where $t = 1, 2, \ldots, 25$), he obtained the following results taking a double logarithmic transformation and using least squares method of estimation:

$$\log \hat{Y}_t = 0.2872 + 0.2882 \log X_t \qquad\qquad r^2 = 0.6556$$
$$(0.0422)$$

The result suggests that approximately two-thirds of interindustry variation in diversification can be explained by variation in research manpower.

Another example would be the estimation of a consumption function from cross-section data on individual households. Household income can be subdivided into appropriate intervals and the average consumption expenditure corresponding to each income range can be calculated. It is often argued that *heteroscedasticity* is more likely to arise in econometric studies using cross-section rather than time-series data. Analysis of microeconomic cross-section data is often concerned with very different individual units, e.g. households with high and low incomes. If data errors are of the same relative importance in the individual household units then the absolute error will be much higher for rich than for poor households. Therefore in, for example, the estimation of a cross-section consumption function there would be a tendency to expect that the variance of the error term would increase with household income. Thus heteroscedasticity might be expected in such cases.

Sources of Statistical Data

In order to be able to test hypotheses in economics using econometric techniques it is obviously first necessary to obtain the appropriate data required, which may be either cross-section or time-series. Regretfully, there is a general ignorance of sources of statistical information among not only economics undergraduates but also some professional economists.

The following list is a sample of some of the principal UK publications of statistical data.

1 *Monthly Digest of Statistics*, published by HMSO and
   including sections on:
   National income and expenditure
   Population statistics
   Labour
   Social services
   Agricultural production
   Production, output and costs
   Fuel and power
   Manufactured goods: chemicals, metals, engineering, vehicles
       and textiles
   Other manufactures
   Construction industry
   Retailing and catering
   Transport sector
   Trade
   Finance
   Wages and prices
   Climatic conditions

2 *Annual Abstract of Statistics*, published by HMSO and
   including sections on:
   Area and climate
   Population statistics
   Social conditions
   Education
   Labour
   Production statistics
   Retail distribution
   Transport and communications
   Trade
   Finance
   National income and expenditure prices

3   *Economic Trends*, a monthly HMSO publication that includes sections on:
Productivity
National income and expenditure
General economic data

4   *Department of Employment Gazette*, a monthly HMSO publication that includes sections on:
Manpower
Employment
Unemployment
Earnings and wage rates
Prices and price indices

5   '*Blue Book*': *National Income and Expenditure*, an HMSO publication with detailed information on national product, income and expenditure.

6   *Bank of England Quarterly Bulletin*, containing general economic data.

DISTRIBUTED LAG MODELS

Consider an aggregate time-series consumption function with a large number of lagged income variables included, e.g.

$$C_t = a + b_0 Y_t + b_1 Y_{t-1} + b_2 Y_{t-2} + \cdots + U_t$$

Let us assign increasingly lower weight or importance to income in past time periods in the form of a series of geometrically declining weights. Hence

$$b_0 = b \qquad b_1 = \lambda b \qquad b_2 = \lambda^2 b \quad \text{etc.}$$

where b is some constant and $0 < \lambda < 1$. Therefore

$$C_t = a + b Y_t + b(\lambda Y_{t-1} + \lambda^2 Y_{t-2} + \cdots) + U_t$$

Lagging all variables one time period and multiplying throughout by λ gives

$$\lambda C_{t-1} = \lambda a + \lambda b(Y_{t-1} + \lambda Y_{t-2} + \cdots) + \lambda U_{t-1}$$
$$= \lambda a + b(\lambda Y_{t-1} + \lambda^2 Y_{t-2} + \cdots) + \lambda U_{t-1}$$

Subtracting and cancelling out yields

$$C_t - \lambda C_{t-1} = a(1 - \lambda) + bY_t + (U_t - \lambda U_{t-1})$$

This result can be rewritten in the following format:

$$C_t = a_1 + bY_t + \lambda C_{t-1} + U_{1t}$$

where a_1, b and λ are constants and U_{1t} is an error term.

This consumption function contains only two explanatory variables: the current value of income (Y_t) and the previous value of consumption (C_{t-1}), which is of course a *lagged endogenous variable*. Therefore the inclusion of a lagged endogenous variable in an equation is equivalent to including a very large number of lagged exogenous variables with geometrically declining weights. The inclusion of a lagged endogenous variable in an equation thus has the important advantage of reducing an equation with a large number of lagged explanatory variables to an equation with a very small number of explanatory variables. Lagged endogenous variables are obviously to be found in models with long adjustment processes where a large number of lagged variables would otherwise have to be included. For example, they are often found in consumption and investment functions.

Consider the following supply equation:

$$q_t = a + bp_t + cq_{t-1} + U_t \tag{1}$$

The presence of a lagged endogenous variable (q_{t-1}) indicates that suppliers are basing output on market price obtained over a long period of time. Although q_{t-1} is an endogenous variable it is a predetermined variable in period t and is therefore treated in much the same way as exogenous variables. If the standard assumptions about the error term are valid then the least squares estimators of the coefficients in equation 1 will have the usual desirable statistical properties.

However, when the error term is serially correlated the estimators of the coefficients in an equation containing only exogenous variables will still be unbiased, although they will not have minimum variance using the OLS method of estimation. Also there will be an underestimate of the variance using least squares formulae. But the least squares estimator of the coefficient of q_{t-1} in equation 1, i.e. $\hat{c}$, will be *biased* when the error term is serially correlated.

The reason for this is as follows. The lagged endogenous variable q_{t-1} is a function of U_{t-1} as seen from the following equation obtained by lagging equation 1 one time period:

$$q_{t-1} = a + bp_{t-1} + cq_{t-2} + U_{t-1}$$

And U_{t-1} is related to U_t because of serial correlation. Hence q_{t-1} is related to U_t. The standard assumption that stated that the error term should be independent of all explanatory variables is therefore violated, since a lagged endogenous variable will not be independent of the error term when serial correlation exists. In this case the OLS estimator of the parameter c in equation 1 will certainly be biased.

It was mentioned earlier, when considering the problem of multicollinearity, that this particular problem can be especially troublesome when examining lag structures. This is due to the obvious close relationship that tends to exist between p_t, p_{t-1}, p_{t-2}, etc. using time-series data. The inclusion of one lagged endogenous variable to replace a number of lagged exogenous variables in a regression equation will thus remove the multicollinearity problem as well as reduce significantly the number of explanatory variables in the regression equation. The drawback occurs when there exists autocorrelation of the error term, since the OLS method will certainly give a biased estimator of the coefficient of the lagged endogenous variable in this case.

The presence of autocorrelated error terms can be tested for by checking the value of the Durbin–Watson statistic (DW) to see whether it differs significantly from a value of 2. If it does then some attempt must be made to reduce the extent of the serial correlation, e.g. by taking first differences. However, it should be noted that the DW test is not strictly speaking applicable to regression equations involving lagged endogenous variables, although it is often applied to such cases for want of anything better.

Exercise 6.1

1   Discuss the properties of the ordinary least squares estimator for the following equations when the error term (U_t) is serially correlated:

   (a) $y_t = a + bx_t + U_t$

   (b) $y_t = a + bx_t + cy_{t-1} + U_t$

2   Explain the rationale for including a lagged endogenous
    variable in a regression equation.
3   Suggest a method for reducing the extent of the serial
    correlation.
4   How would you test for the presence of serially correlated
    error terms?

Exercise 6.2

1   Explain the logic of the first-order autoregressive process for
    generating error terms, i.e.

$$U_t = cU_{t-1} + E_t$$

where U_t is the value of the error term in period t and E_t is a
completely random series. That is, no relationship whatsoever
exists between the value of E_t in this period and its value in any
previous period.

2   Use the above equation to explain roughly why the presence of
    autocorrelated error terms produces biased estimates when
    lagged endogenous variables are present, e.g. in the
    relationship

$$y_t = bx_t + cy_{t-1} + U_t$$

3   In what sort of economic relationship would lagged variables
    be included?

DUMMY VARIABLES

Finally let us briefly consider the use of dummy variables in
econometrics. Dummy variables can only take two values: 0 or 1.
They stand for the presence or absence of certain effects that
influence the dependent variable in a regression equation. They are
treated as any other exogenous variable, and their coefficients are
estimated from the usual least squares formulae. Let us consider
two examples of the use of dummy variables, the first using
time-series data and the second using cross-section data.

Dummy variables are often included in time-series data to allow
for seasonal effects. Assume that the same relationship holds for
all seasons except for certain effects that result in a change in the
constant term of a regression equation. For example, in the case of
seasonal variations in icecream sales demand will clearly be higher

during the summer months than during the winter months, for a given price charged. This implies that the constant term in the demand equation should be greater in value during the summer period. To allow for this the dummy variable D can be included in the demand equation to give

$$Q_t = a + bP_t + cD_t + U_t$$

where $D_t = 0$ when winter data is used and $D_t = 1$ when summer data is used. The coefficient c on the dummy variable D is specified *a priori* to be positive. Consequently the intercept of the demand equation on the quantity (vertical) axis of a plot will equal a during the winter months and $(a + c)$ during the summer period, as illustrated in Figure 6.1.

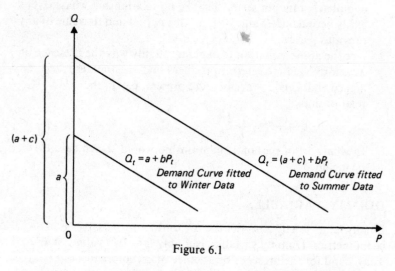

Figure 6.1

A second example using cross-section data is that of an individual's salary being dependent upon age and professional and academic qualifications. It might be expected that an individual's salary would tend to be higher, *ceteris paribus*, if he or she had a degree or professional qualification. Let the dummy variable $D_t = 0$ if the individual has no such qualification, and let $D_t = 1$ if the individual possesses a degree or professional qualification. Hence the form of the model is

$$S_t = a + bA_t + cD_t + U_t$$

where S_t is the tth individual's salary and A_t is the tth individual's age. It is specified *a priori* that the coefficient c on the dummy variable will be positive, which will make an individual's salary higher if he or she is qualified at any given age.

The advantages of using dummy variables are that they reduce the number of separate regressions to be performed and that they allow all of the observations to be used together to estimate the coefficients a and b.

Chapter 7

Empirical Studies in Macroeconomics

In this chapter consideration will be given to some of the important applied studies in macroeconomics and to interpretation of the findings. Controversy surrounds the actual interpretation in many cases, and an attempt will be made to outline the arguments and counterarguments put forward. My personal opinion will also be indicated in such cases, which no doubt some will wish to disagree with.

Four principal study areas will be analysed: wage and price inflation; monetary policy; investment expenditure; and the consumption function. All the empirical results that will be presented in regression format in this chapter have been obtained by using the OLS method of estimation.

WAGE AND PRICE INFLATION

The Phillips Curve

The inevitable starting point in a study of wage and price inflation is the Phillips curve (or in the beginning there was the Phillips curve). In 1958 Phillips published his famous article studying the relationship between unemployment and the rate of change of money wage rates in the UK for 1861–1957. Since that time every economics undergraduate has been introduced to the notion of the Phillips curve and the debate concerning cost-push versus demand-pull theories of inflation. Let us first consider the statistical method used by Phillips to obtain his famous curve.

Phillips's initial hypothesis was that variations in the rate of change of money wage rates in the UK could be adequately explained by variations in the level of unemployment and the rate of change of unemployment. To test this theory he first considered the period 1861–1913. He constructed a scatter diagram for this period using UK annual data, with the average rate of change of money wage rates during the year presented on the vertical axis and average unemployment during the year on the horizontal axis. He then calculated the average values of the rate of change of money wage rates and of percentage unemployment in those years in which unemployment lay in the intervals 0–2, 2–3, 3–4, 4–5, 5–7 and 7–11% respectively (the upper bound being included in each interval). These 6 pairs of values were denoted by crosses on the scatter diagram.

Phillips believed that each cross would give an approximation to the rate of change of wages that would be associated with the indicated level of unemployment if unemployment was held constant at that level. His rationale for this belief was that each interval would include some years in which unemployment was increasing and some in which it was decreasing, so that by a process of cancelling out each cross would give an approximation to the rate of change of wages that would be associated with a particular level of unemployment if unemployment were held constant at that level. Phillips then proceeded to fit a curve through these 6 crosses, which has become known as the Phillips curve. He imposed this curve as fitted to the 1861–1913 data on to scatter diagrams for the later periods 1913–48 and 1948–57. However, there was no evidence of a strong relationship between unemployment and the rate of change of money wage rates during these two periods.

Several points of interest and criticism arise out of the way in which Phillips fitted the curve to his data. Surely in accordance with his initial hypothesis he should have carried out a multiple regression of ΔW (the rate of change of money wage rates) on U (percentage unemployment) and ΔU (the rate of change in U) for each of the periods he was interested in. I am very dubious about the statistical validity of the method adopted by Phillips of averaging out the data to leave him with only 6 observations. Furthermore, Phillips gave no indication of the goodness of fit of the relationship he attempted to establish. If he had used a conventional multiple regression procedure this would have yielded a multiple correlation coefficient to indicate goodness of fit and estimated standard errors from which t-ratios or confidence intervals could be computed etc.

The form of the equation chosen by Phillips was

$$\Delta W_t + a = bU_t^c$$

or, taking a double logarithmic transformation of the variables,

$$\log (\Delta W_t + a) = \log b + c \log U_t$$

where a, b and c are constants. In fact a is a positive constant included simply to make the rate of change of money wage rates positive in every year to which the data applied, since the logarithm of a negative number is impossible. Phillips's conclusion that inflation was primarily of the demand-pull variety in the UK over the period 1861–1957 because of the statistical evidence he presented is in my opinion a very dubious one.

He used percentage unemployment (U) as a proxy variable for excess supply of labour, and the demand-pull theory of inflation is based upon the notion that it is excess demand for labour that causes wage rates to rise. Hence according to Phillips the demand-pull model should yield a negative correlation between the rate of change of money wage rates and percentage unemployment. It is certainly true to say that a more accurate measure of proportional excess demand for labour would be $(V - U)$, where V is the proportional extent of vacancies. However, vacancy data is not generally considered to be very reliable, and therefore U rather than $(V - U)$ has been used in empirical studies.

I have tested for some evidence of a postwar Phillips curve for the UK economy using annual data for the years 1949–68 inclusive. I first tested for a simple linear relationship between ΔW and U, giving

$$\Delta W_t = 6\cdot88 - 0\cdot878U_t \qquad\qquad (1)$$
$$(1\cdot07) \qquad\qquad r^2 = 0\cdot036 \qquad DW = 1\cdot65$$

(where the estimated standard error is given in brackets as usual, and where the DW statistic indicates that the test showed no autocorrelation at the 5% probability level). The result clearly shows no evidence of a simple linear relationship.

However, this could be explained by the fact that Phillips

clearly believed this relationship to be nonlinear in format although he believed it to be linear in logarithms. I accordingly applied a double logarithmic transformation to the variables ΔW and U and regressed $\log \Delta W$ on $\log U$, giving

$$\log \Delta W_t = 1\cdot39 + 0\cdot198 \log U_t \tag{2}$$
$$(0\cdot489) \qquad r^2 = 0\cdot0086 \qquad DW = 1\cdot15$$

(The DW statistic indicates that the test showed positive autocorrelation at the 5% probability level.) This result is even worse and suggests that only $0\cdot86\%$ of the total variation in money wage rates in the UK could be accounted for by annual variation in percentage unemployment over the period 1949–68.

Finally, returning to the linear format I included the variable ΔU together with U in the regression equation in accordance with Phillips's initial hypothesis. Phillips believed that ΔU and ΔW would be negatively correlated, indicating that the rate of change of money wage rates would be higher during those years in which percentage unemployment was falling than when it was rising, for any given value of percentage unemployment. My results were

$$\Delta W_t = 7\cdot75 - 1\cdot39U_t + 0\cdot885\Delta U_t \tag{3}$$
$$(1\cdot31) \quad (1\cdot25)$$
$$R^2 = 0\cdot0636 \qquad DW = 1\cdot62$$

(The DW statistic indicates that the test showed no autocorrelation at the 5% probability level.) The sign of the estimated coefficient of ΔU_t is incorrect and in addition equation 3 suggests that only $6\cdot36\%$ of total variation in money wage rates could be explained by variations in percentage unemployment and the rate of change of percentage unemployment during this postwar period.

The results as given by equations 1, 2 and 3 indicate that there is no evidence whatsoever for the existence of a stable Phillips curve in the UK during the postwar period. It is my personal opinion that the Phillips curve is mere fantasy and not reality. Nevertheless, certain economists are still attempting to defend the notion of a Phillips curve by searching for a deeper understanding of Phillips's work than the simplistic method he advanced in his original article in 1958 (see, for example, Desai, 1975).

Cost-push Theories

Let us now consider cost-push theories of inflation. The cost-push theory most commonly presented is that money wage rates rise because of trade union power or pushfulness. Most of the early empirical work related this pushing to the proportional rate of change in the retail price index (ΔP). The rationale for this is that trade unions base their wage claims on the rise that occurs in the cost of living in any given year. For example, Lipsey (1960), studying the relation between unemployment and the rate of change of money wage rates in the UK for 1862–1957, obtained the following estimated wage equation using annual UK data for 1923–57, excluding war years:

$$\Delta W_t = 0.74 + 0.43 U_t^{-1} + 11.18 U_t^{-4} + 0.034 \Delta U_t + 0.69 \Delta P_t$$
$$(2.1) \qquad (6.0) \qquad (0.012) \qquad (0.08)$$
$$R^2 = 0.91$$

The equation clearly fits the data very well as indicated by the very high value of the multiple correlation coefficient.

The interesting question here is whether it is the three variables representing demand-pull pressures (U^{-1}, U^{-4} and ΔU) or the cost-push variable (ΔP) that is most important in explaining variations in wage rates over the period covered in Lipsey's study. By computing t-ratios for the estimated coefficients it can be discovered which variables are most significant in this respect. From Table 7.1 it can be seen that the variables U^{-1} and U^{-4} are

Table 7.1

Variable	t-ratio
U^{-1}	0.205
U^{-4}	1.86
ΔU	2.83
ΔP	8.63

clearly insignificant at the 5% probability level since their t-ratios are less than 2. The remaining demand-pull variable ΔU is just significant, but its coefficient has the wrong sign since it should be a negative value. Hence the only important explanatory variable in this wage equation is the cost-push variable ΔP, which has the correct sign and a very high and significant t-ratio of 8.63.

I included ΔP into my postwar wage equation together with U and obtained the following estimated equation:

$$\Delta W_t = 2\cdot43 + 0\cdot0597U_t + 0\cdot79\Delta P_t \qquad (4)$$
$$(0\cdot835) \qquad (0\cdot203)$$
$$R^2 = 0\cdot492 \qquad DW = 1\cdot86$$

(The DW statistic indicates that the test showed no autocorrelation at the 5% probability level.) As before, the unemployment variable (U) is insignificant and has the wrong sign. The price variable (ΔP) on the other hand is significant (t-ratio = $3\cdot9$), and its sign is correct. The result is a considerable improvement on equations 1, 2 and 3 which all contain only demand-pull explanatory variables.

However, the price variable clearly does not perform as well as in Lipsey's estimated equation using earlier data, as indicated by the lower values of the t-ratio and of R^2. This suggests that postwar variations in wage rates are more difficult to explain than those during the interwar years in the UK. To test this view I estimated the same wage equation using interwar data for 1921–38 inclusive, giving

$$\Delta W_t = -0\cdot526 + 0\cdot0679U_t + 1\cdot07\Delta P_t \qquad (5)$$
$$(0\cdot264) \qquad (0\cdot175)$$
$$R^2 = 0\cdot72 \qquad DW = 1\cdot27$$

(The DW statistic indicates that the test was inconclusive at the 5% probability level.) This result supports my view since R^2 has increased from 0·492 to 0·72 and the t-ratio of ΔP has also increased, from 3·9 to 6·1. Note that the unemployment variable U once again has the wrong sign and is clearly insignificant (t-ratio = $0\cdot257$).

All the results presented so far using econometric techniques firmly reject the demand-pull theory and give some support to the alternative cost-push theory. However, caution is needed in interpreting these results because an association between wage increases and price rises is not inconsistent with the demand-pull theory of inflation. A rise in demand for goods will lead to a rise in price and output according to basic microeconomic theory, which will in turn result in an increased demand for labour and other factors of production and pull-up wage rates. What is difficult, if not impossible, for the demand-pull theory to explain is

why this pulling-up of wages does not show up at all in the
creation of excess demand for labour, as measured by variations in
percentage unemployment. Incidentally, Phillips took the relevant
figure on the cost side in wage negotiations to be the annual
percentage increase in the retail price incex, and he used this as a
measure of the cost-push element in wage negotiations.

Friedman's Price Expectations Model

The price expectations model of Friedman (1968) could provide
some validity for the demand-pull hypothesis. The general
argument is that the price variable in the wage equation is a proxy
variable for the influence of price anticipations on wage offers and
aspirations. In terms of this explanation, observers in Britain are
not seeing the replacement of the demand-pull phenomena by a
cost-push process of wage and price inflation caused by increased
trade union militancy and greater monopoly power in British
industry. Instead they are seeing people's anticipations of price
changes adapting to the postwar phenomenon of overfull
employment and slow inflation. However, Solow (1969) in an
empirical study of the postwar UK and US economies found no
evidence to suggest that Friedman's expectations model is valid in
Britain.

Hines's Theory of Trade Union Pushfulness

Finally, let us consider the most famous and controversial of the
cost-push theories of inflation, which was made by Hines (1964)
in a study of trade unions and wage inflation in the UK for
1893–1961. Briefly, Hines successfully showed that his measure of
trade union pushfulness, i.e. the percentage of the labour force
unionised (T) and more especially the rate of change of this
variable over a given year (ΔT), makes a statistically significant
contribution towards explaining annual variation in wage rates.
Unlike Phillips, Hines produced direct econometric evidence to
support his hypothesis. He took ΔT as an index of trade union
pushfulness under the assumption that when unions are being
aggressive they simultaneously increase their membership and bid
up wages.

The following equations were all estimated by the OLS method using annual UK data over the period 1921–61 (excluding war years) and are a sample of Hines's results, where the variables used are defined as follows:

ΔW_t = % rate of change of an index of money wage rates.

T_t = % of labour force unionised.

$\Delta T_t = T_t - T_{t-1}$ = rate of change of % of labour force unionised.

U_t = % of labour force unemployed.

ΔU_t = rate of change of % of labour force unemployed.

ΔP_t = % rate of change of the retail price index.

ΔM_t = % rate of change of an index of import prices.

ΔX_t = % rate of change of an index of productivity per man-year.

t = time subscript denoting tth year (where $(t - \tfrac{1}{2})$ indicates a lag of six months).

$$\Delta W_t = 2\cdot423 + 2\cdot763\Delta T_t \tag{6}$$
$$(0\cdot272)$$
$$r^2 = 0\cdot7682$$

$$\Delta W_t = -7\cdot36 + 2\cdot922\Delta T_t + 0\cdot311T_t \tag{7}$$
$$(0\cdot173) \qquad (0\cdot045)$$
$$R^2 = 0\cdot9069 \qquad DW = 1\cdot57$$

$$\Delta W_t = 1\cdot159 + 1\cdot96\Delta T_t + 0\cdot07T_t + 0\cdot386\Delta P_{t-\frac{1}{2}} - 0\cdot16U_t \tag{8}$$
$$(0\cdot34) \qquad (0\cdot12) \quad (0\cdot12) \qquad\qquad (0\cdot14)$$
$$R^2 = 0\cdot9197 \qquad DW = 1\cdot17$$

$$\Delta P_t = -0\cdot234 + 0\cdot586\Delta W_t + 0\cdot084\Delta M_{t-\frac{1}{2}} - 0\cdot004\Delta X_t \tag{9}$$
$$(0\cdot082) \qquad (0\cdot044) \qquad\quad (0\cdot179)$$
$$R^2 = 0\cdot8963 \qquad DW = 1\cdot21$$

(The DW statistics indicate that, at the 1% probability level, the test showed no autocorrelation for equation 7 and was inconclusive for equations 8 and 9.)

Equation 6 suggests that approximately 77% of total variation in money wage rates could be accounted for by variation in ΔT, which is taken to be a proxy variable for trade union pushfulness on wage demands. The fit is somewhat improved in equation 7 when the variable T is also included, since the R^2 is increased from 0·7682 to 0·9069. However, in equation 8, where the additional explanatory variables ΔP and U are included, the variable T is clearly insignificant at the 5% probability level. The only significant variables in equation 8 are ΔT and ΔP with

t-ratios of 5·76 and 3·22 respectively. Therefore Hines's results suggest that the cost-push variables ΔT and ΔP can together explain variations in wage rates over the period 1921–61 very successfully, where ΔT is the most important explanatory variable. The estimated price equation, equation 9, suggests that wage rates were the most important determinant of price changes. Surprisingly the import price variable (ΔM) is just insignificant, and even more surprisingly the productivity variable (ΔX) is clearly insignificant at the 5% probability level. Hines's results will be returned to in the following chapter, when alternative methods of estimation for dealing with this interdependence that exists between wages and prices will be considered.

I tested the performance of Hines's cost-push variable in several estimated wage equations using annual UK data for the interwar period 1921–38 and for the postwar period 1949–68. The results from employing the OLS method of estimation were as follows:

For the interwar period, 1921–38,
$$\Delta W_t = 0.1155 + 2.446\Delta T_t \tag{10}$$
$$(0.1783)$$
$$r^2 = 0.9217 \qquad DW = 1.48$$

$$\Delta W_t = 0.8525 + 2.424\Delta T_t - 0.03T_t \tag{11}$$
$$(0.2274) \qquad (0.178)$$
$$R^2 = 0.9218 \qquad DW = 1.50$$

$$\Delta W_t = 13.3 - 0.26U_t + 0.22\Delta U_t + 0.26\Delta P_t - 0.38T_t + 1.77\Delta T_t \tag{12}$$
$$(0.19) \quad (0.26) \quad (0.16) \quad (0.24) \quad (0.40)$$
$$R^2 = 0.9482 \qquad DW = 1.19$$

For the postwar period, 1949–68,
$$\Delta W_t = 5.691 + 3.667\Delta T_t \tag{13}$$
$$(0.8162)$$
$$r^2 = 0.5286 \qquad DW = 2.36$$

$$\Delta W_t = 13.07 + 3.762\Delta T_t - 0.1859T_t \tag{14}$$
$$(0.8741) \qquad (0.497)$$
$$R^2 = 0.5325 \qquad DW = 2.40$$

$$\Delta W_t = 20.1 - 0.28U_t + 0.23\Delta U_t + 0.52\Delta P_t - 0.4T_t + 2.87\Delta T_t \tag{15}$$
$$(1.0) \quad (0.90) \quad (0.21) \quad (0.47) \quad (0.85)$$
$$R^2 = 0.7316 \qquad DW = 2.19$$

(The DW statistics indicate, at the 5% probability level, that the test showed no autocorrelation for equations 10, 13 and 14 and was inconclusive for equations 11, 12 and 15.)

These results present strong statistical support for Hines's hypothesis, especially during the interwar period in the UK. Equation 10 suggests that over 92% of total variation in money wage rates in the UK during the period 1921–38 could be explained by variation in Hines's cost-push variable (ΔT) alone. The corresponding result for the postwar period, as given by equation 13, indicates that only approximately 53% of total variation in money wage rates could be explained by variation in ΔT alone. The t-ratio for ΔT in equation 10 is 13·72, whereas its corresponding value in equation 13 is 4·49.

The inclusion of the variable T in equations 11 and 14 for the interwar and postwar periods respectively made no improvement to the fit. In both cases the coefficient of this variable was clearly insignificant at the 5% probability level, and in addition the sign was incorrect. Finally, in equations 12 and 15 for the interwar and postwar periods respectively all the principal demand-pull and cost-push variables were simultaneously included into the wage equation. The results clearly show that the only significant variable during the interwar years was ΔT and that for the postwar period only the variables ΔP and ΔT were significant, although once again ΔT was the most powerful explanatory variable present in the wage equation.

The tentative conclusion to be drawn from these results is that in the interwar years ΔT can adequately explain variations in wage rates independently of price changes or any other effects, whereas in the postwar years ΔT and ΔP appear to have each made a separate contribution to adequately explaining variations in wage rates, although ΔT is the more significant or important of these two explanatory variables. These results basically corroborate the results presented by Hines and firmly reject the demand-pull theories of wage inflation for the interwar and postwar periods in the UK.

Nevertheless, a considerable proportion of economists still view Hines's results with scepticism. The case against his findings has basically centred on two points of criticism. The first is that the correlation is spurious because there is no well-grounded theory of union behaviour underlying Hines's hypothesis. I strongly reject this viewpoint. Trade union membership and trade union power in wage bargaining have increased steadily since the beginning of this century, and the results reflect this commonsense view. I do not personally regard these results as necessarily implying blame or criticism of trade union behaviour. Instead Hines's results simply illustrate that trade unions have been highly successful in raising the wages of their members since the end of the First World War, and those who reject Hines's findings are in effect saying that trade unions have been totally unsuccessful in raising the living standards of their members!

The second point of criticism raised is that the causality in any relationship between ΔW and ΔT runs from ΔW to ΔT. It has been argued that workers may incorrectly ascribe a wage rise to trade union activity and then join the unions and pay the membership fees out of gratitude for services they wrongly believe the unions have rendered. I think it is more plausible that the causality runs from ΔT to ΔW as Hines believed, since this second criticism implies that workers are continuously misled into believing that their wage rise is due to trade union activity! No doubt the controversy concerning demand-pull and cost-push inflation will continue, and I can only leave the student to draw his or her own conclusions about the relative merits of these opposing views.

MONETARY POLICY

Keynesian Theory

Keynesian macroeconomics, as represented by the conventional IS–LM curve diagram, suggests that monetary policy has a role to play in determining the equilibrium levels of national income and interest rates in the economy. For example, an increase in the supply of money will have the effect of bidding up the price of bonds and hence reducing interest rates. This in turn may result in an increase in investment expenditure, since the present value of the stream of revenues from any investment project will vary inversely with interest rates, and via the multiplier this will have a multiple effect on the level of national income. Figure 7.1 shows diagrammatically the effect of an increase in the supply of money on the equilibrium levels of national income (Y) and the market rate of interest (r). The effect is shown by a shift to the

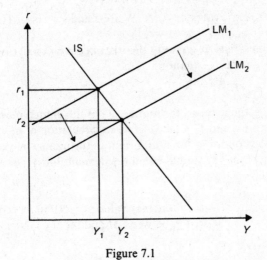

Figure 7.1

right of the LM curve, resulting in an increase in Y from Y_1 to Y_2 and a fall in r from r_1 to r_2.

Keynesians believe, however, that monetary policy is not as powerful a tool for controlling the economy as fiscal policy, because monetary policy affects national income via an indirect route, i.e.

$$\text{money supply} \underset{-}{\longrightarrow} \text{rate of interest} \underset{-}{\longrightarrow} \text{investment} \underset{+}{\longrightarrow} \text{income}$$

In addition, most empirical studies suggest that there is little or no evidence of a relationship existing between investment expenditure and interest rates. The determinants of investment will be considered more fully in the following section.

Monetarist View

On the other hand, the monetarists believe that 'money matters'. Money is considered to be the only important determinant of national income, and they call upon econometric evidence to support their claim. Milton Friedman is probably the best known and most fervent supporter of the monetarist view. In this country Enoch Powell and Sir Keith Joseph have both given strong support to the monetarist view, as well as many famous economists, e.g. Professor A. A. Walters and Professor H. Johnson.

The monetarists or quantity theorists begin by analysing the classic statement or equation:

$$M_d V = PT$$

where M_d is the demand for money, PT is the annual money value of transactions, and V is the velocity of circulation of money.

Given the condition for equilibrium in the money market: that the supply of money should equal the demand for it, i.e.

$$M_s = M_d (= M)$$

and given that PT is the monetary value of GNP in an economy, then there is a relationship between M and money GNP:

$$MV = GNP$$

or

$$V = GNP/M$$

The reciprocal of V has become known as the Cambridge 'k' and is simply the ratio of the money supply to GNP, i.e.

$$k = M/GNP$$

The general view held by the monetarists is that V (and hence k) is constant. The implication of this is that the ratio of the supply of money to GNP is constant, and the monetarists believe that the chain of causality runs from the money supply to GNP, so that an increase (decrease) of $X\%$ in the supply of money will cause a corresponding increase (decrease) of $X\%$ in GNP.

Walters's Study of Money Supply and GNP

Let us consider and analyse the results obtained by Walters (1971).

(1)   In accordance with the monetarist view Walters studied the behaviour of k using annual UK data for 1881–1967 in order to consider its stability, which is so important to the monetarists. He discovered considerable short term instability in k. As a measure of the variability in k Walters used the *coefficient of variation*, which records the standard deviation as a percentage of the mean

Table 7.2

	1877–1913	*1920–38*	*1951–61*
Mean value of k	0·51	0·65	0·63
Coefficient of variation (%)	6	9	13

value. He produced the results in Table 7.2 for three subperiods.

The implications of these results is that approximately one out of every three values of k recorded for the years 1877–1913 lay more than 6 percentage points from the mean value and that this figure increased to 9 percentage points during the interwar years and to 13 percentage points during the 1950s in the UK. Walters regarded this as an 'abysmal' result for the monetarist view of the economy. The monetarist view is clearly discredited.

(2)   In accordance with the Keynesian theory Walters investigated the relationship between the Cambridge 'k' and the market rate of interest. Using annual UK data for 1880–1961 he obtained the following results:

$$\log k_t = -1·21 - 0·2 \log r_t + 0·29 \log Y_{r_t} \qquad (16)$$
$$\qquad\quad (0·08) \qquad (0·04)$$
$$R^2 = 0·40$$

$$\Delta \log k_t = 0·0049 - 0·45 \Delta \log r_t - 0·67 \Delta \log Y_{r_t} \qquad (17)$$
$$\qquad\quad (0·09) \qquad\quad (0·22)$$
$$R^2 = 0·33$$

where Y_r is real income and r is the yield on consols.

Equation 16 suggests that 40% of total variation in k over the period 1880–1961 could be accounted for by variation in interest rates and real income. Although the fit is not particularly good the coefficients of both explanatory variables are significant at the 5% probability level (the t-ratios for r and Y_r being 2·5 and 7·25 respectively). Clearly the level of real income is the more significant of the explanatory variables.

Recall from chapter 4 that when a double logarithmic transformation of the data is taken the negative of the estimated coefficient is an estimate of the elasticity of the dependent variable on the explanatory variable concerned. Hence 0·2 represents an estimate of the elasticity of k on the rate of interest. Allowing for the possibility that the correlation may be due to trends in the basic data, Walters took first differences to analyse year-to-year changes in these variables. The results, as given by equation 17, indicate an even lower R^2 of 0·33, so that two-thirds of total variation in the dependent variable cannot be accounted for by variations in the explanatory variables. Once again the coefficients of both explanatory variables are significant at the 5% probability level (the *t*-ratios for r and Y_r being 5·0 and 3·04 respectively). Therefore in equation 17 the rate of interest is the more significant of the two explanatory variables in terms of *t*-ratios. Note also that the positive relationship between k and real income that existed in equation 16 has become a negative association between changes or first differences.

Equations 16 and 17 both indicate a negative correlation between k and the rate of interest. Consider the implications of this for the efficacy of monetary policy in the UK. The quantity equation can be written as

$$M = k \times GNP$$

It follows that the effectiveness of monetary policy will be diminished the greater is the degree of positive correlation between the stock of money (M) and k. From the conventional IS–LM curve diagram a rise (fall) in the supply of money will result in a fall (rise) in interest rates. But Walters's results suggest that a fall (rise) in interest rates will result in a rise (fall) in k. Thus M and k indeed appear to be positively correlated.

(3)   Walters next considered the relationship that exists between GNP and the stock of money. He allowed for the possibility of a substantial lag in the response of the economy to changes in the quantity of money. He related the change in money income to changes in the stock of money in current and earlier periods. The results for each of the time periods he considered were as follows:

1880–1913

$$\Delta \log Y_t = 0.0042 + 0.43 \, \Delta \log M_t + 0.45 \, \Delta \log M_{t-1}$$
$$(0.28) \qquad\qquad (0.28)$$
$$- \, 0.132 \, \Delta \log M_{t-2} \qquad\qquad\qquad (18)$$
$$(0.22)$$
$$R^2 = 0.29$$

1922–38

$$\Delta \log Y_t = -0.0021 + 0.79 \, \Delta \log M_t + 0.59 \, \Delta \log M_{t-1}$$
$$ (0.41) (0.45)$$
$$ - 0.39 \, \Delta \log M_{t-2} \tag{19}$$
$$ (0.31)$$
$$R^2 = 0.52$$

1948–66

$$\Delta \log Y_t = \text{constant} + 0.537 \, \Delta \log M_t + 0.046 \, \Delta \log M_{t-1} \tag{20}$$
$$\phantom{\Delta \log Y_t = \text{constant} +} (0.543) (0.544)$$
$$R^2 = 0.156$$

where Y_t is GNP or income at current prices in year t.

The results are clearly very poor, particularly for the postwar period. The general case advanced by Keynesian economists against the monetarists has centred on the 'causation' argument. Kaldor (1970) regarded the money supply as being endogenous rather than exogenous in any regression of Y_t on M_t. In other words, he considered the direction of causality as running from Y_t to M_t. When GNP increases the resulting increased demand for money evokes an increase in supply. The government varies the supply of money to meet the needs of trade with the possible objective of stabilising interest rates at some desired level.

This brings the argument back to the important point that correlation does not imply causality. However, in this case Walters's results for the recent postwar period show very little evidence of any relationship between year-to-year changes in GNP and the supply of money in the UK. Walters considered some attempts at explanations for his very poor results, including the possibility that the statistics are wrong. However, he was forced to concede that 'the explanations are simply not satisfactory'. It must have been painful for a monetarist to draw such conclusions! It appears to me that, on the basis of Walters's extensive study, only the following factual information is left concerning the efficacy of monetary policy in the UK:

1 The results presented by Walters reveal no close short run relationship between changes in the money supply and changes in GNP.
2 Any relationship that may exist does not in any case imply causality.

It appears that 'money does *not* matter' in the UK.

INVESTMENT EXPENDITURE

This section will consider four different models of investment and analyse their success in explaining variations in aggregate investment expenditure (ignoring initially the government sector and investment in housing and inventories) in the UK using postwar data. Hence it will be considering the explanation of movements in private-sector nondwelling gross-fixed-capital formation.

Accelerator Model

The accelerator principle is pre-Keynesian in origin and can be traced back to Aftalion (1909). A crude or naive form of the accelerator model was set out by Clark (1917), which stated that the desired level of the capital stock (K) is proportional to the level of output produced (O), i.e.

$$K_t^* = vO_t$$

where v is a constant and K_t^* and O_t are respectively the desired capital stock and the output produced in period t. Now gross investment is made up of net investment plus replacement investment. Net investment only takes place when there is a wish to increase the capital stock. Hence

$$\Delta K_t = v \, \Delta O_t$$

In other words, net investment is proportional to the change in output that takes place over the time period concerned.

Clark himself raised the following criticisms of his crude accelerator model:

1   The accelerator is inoperative (or at least not fully operative) when excess capacity exists.
2   There should be lags present in the model due to the delay between the ordering of capital goods and actual delivery. In other words businessmen are forced to base their capital stock requirements on past levels of output.
3   In the real world the data collected refers to gross investment rather than net.

In separate studies by Chenery (1952) and Goodwin (1951) this very naive accelerator model was accordingly amended to take into account criticisms 2 and 3 above. Hence the investment function has the form

$$I_t = f(\Delta O_t, \Delta O_{t-1}, \Delta O_{t-2}) + I_{R_t}$$

where I_t is *gross* investment and I_{R_t} is *replacement* investment in period t. Replacement investment depends upon the age and size of the capital stock, and a common assumption is to set

$$I_{R_t} = dK_{t-1}$$

assuming a lag of one period, where d is the proportion of the capital stock replaced each time period.

Under the assumption of a linear format for this accelerator model, an equation of the following form is obtained:

$$I_t = k + a\,\Delta O_t + b\,\Delta O_{t-1} + c\,\Delta O_{t-2} + dK_{t-1} + U_t$$

where a, b, c, d and k are the parameters to be estimated from a set of data and U_t is the error term in period t.

Wynn and Holden (1974, chapter 2) tested various investment models. They used UK annual data for 1955–70, and their source of data was the '*Blue Book*': *National Income and Expenditure*. Their version of Chenery's accelerator model that best explained variations in investment over the period concerned (ignoring more complex lag structures) was

$$I_t = 0{\cdot}5842 + 0{\cdot}0302\Delta O_t + 0{\cdot}0394\Delta O_{t-1} + 0{\cdot}0195\Delta O_{t-2}$$
$$\quad (0{\cdot}0969) \quad (0{\cdot}0103) \qquad (0{\cdot}009) \qquad\qquad (0{\cdot}0106)$$
$$\quad + 0{\cdot}0586K_{t-1}$$
$$\quad (0{\cdot}0041)$$

$$R^2 = 0{\cdot}9641$$

All the estimated coefficients in the above equation satisfy the *a priori* conditions of being positive, and with the exception of the variable ΔO_{t-2} all other variables are significant at the 5% probability level, as seen from the computed t-ratios given in Table 7.3. Clearly K_{t-1} is the most significant of the explanatory variables as measured in terms of t-ratios. It was mentioned in chapter 4 that multicollinearity can be particularly troublesome when considering lag structures and that the consequences of this phenomenon will be relatively high estimated standard errors for

Table 7.3

Variable	t-ratio
ΔO_t	2·932
ΔO_{t-1}	4·378
ΔO_{t-2}	1·840
K_{t-1}	14·29

the coefficients concerned. Hence multicollinearity accounts for the relatively low *t*-ratios for the coefficients of ΔO_t, ΔO_{t-1} and ΔO_{t-2} to some extent. The very high value for the multiple correlation coefficient indicates that 96·41% of annual variation in investment expenditure can be accounted for by this accelerator model. This is clearly an excellent fit to the data. Accelerator models do, however, ignore the financial considerations facing firms. For example, a shortage of funds for investment purposes may prevent the desired level of the capital stock from being achieved. This leads to a consideration of liquidity.

Liquidity Models of Investment

Lund (1971) suggested that the desired level of the capital stock depends upon the liquidity conditions facing the firm. Assuming a proportional relationship,

$$K_t^* = bL_t$$

where L_t, the liquidity in period t, may be represented by (gross profits after taxation plus depreciation minus dividends paid out). This yields a general liquidity model of the form

$$I_t = f(\Delta L_t, \Delta L_{t-1}, \Delta L_{t-2}) + I_{R_t}$$

where

$$\Delta L_t = (L_t - L_{t-1}) \qquad I_{R_t} = dK_{t-1}$$

Wynn and Holden (1974) found that the most successful linear equation for this liquidity model using the same UK annual data for 1955–70 was

$$I_t = 0.5598 + 0.1495\Delta L_t + 0.372\Delta L_{t-1} + 0.1561\Delta L_{t-2}$$
$$(0.1561) \quad (0.1324) \qquad (0.1401) \qquad (0.133)$$
$$+ \ 0.0707K_{t-1}$$
$$(0.0064)$$

$$R^2 = 0.9133 \qquad DW = 1.42$$

where L_t is the undistributed income (after taxation) of companies divided by a price index of fixed assets. (The DW statistic indicates that the test was inconclusive at the 5% probability level.)

In this instance the coefficients of only two of the explanatory variables are significant at the 5% probability level, i.e. ΔL_{t-1} and K_{t-1}, as can be seen from the t-ratios given in Table 7.4. Once

Table 7.4

Variable	t-ratio
ΔL_t	1·13
ΔL_{t-1}	2·66
ΔL_{t-2}	1·17
K_{t-1}	11·05

again K_{t-1} is clearly the most significant of the explanatory variables, and the problem of multicollinearity explains the very low t-ratios for the coefficients of ΔL_t, ΔL_{t-1} and ΔL_{t-2} to some degree. The multiple correlation coefficient indicates that 91·33% of annual variation in investment expenditure can be accounted for by this liquidity model. This suggests a very good fit to the data. However, it is slightly inferior to the accelerator model.

Profits Model of Investment

Grunfeld (1960) suggested that future expected profits would play an important role in determining investment expenditure, and he proposed the stock market valuation of a company as an appropriate measure. Assuming a proportional relationship between the desired level of the capital stock and a measure of the stock market valuation of a company (K_t^* and V_t respectively at period t) yields

$$K_t^* = bV_t$$

which in turn gives an investment function of the form

$$I_t = f(\Delta V_t, \Delta V_{t-1}, \Delta V_{t-2}) + I_{R_t}$$

where

$$\Delta V_t = (V_t - V_{t-1}) \qquad I_{R_t} = dK_{t-1}$$

This is a microeconomic investment function for an individual firm. In order to aggregate, the stock market valuation of a company has to be replaced by the average value of the *Financial Times* share-price index during a given year (S_t).

Wynn and Holden (1974) discovered that the highest R^2 obtainable for this profits model was 0·9141, using UK annual data for 1955–70 as before. The only significant variables were ΔS_{t-1} and K_{t-1}, which had *t*-ratios of 2·33 and 10·47 respectively.

Wynn and Holden discovered that the accelerator model performed best of all in explaining variations in UK aggregate investment over the period 1955–70. However, it is apparent that all the various models tested performed very well in terms of R^2 and that the lagged capital stock variable (K_{t-1}) was the most highly significant of the explanatory variables in all the models considered.

One important explanatory variable in terms of Keynesian macroeconomics that has been absent from all the investment equations thus far considered is the rate of interest. The Keynesian inverse relationship between interest rates and investment expenditure gives the IS schedule its negative slope. If investment was completely interest-inelastic, then the IS curve would become a straight line parallel to the vertical axis. The implication of this in terms of conventional Keynesian macroeconomics would be that changing the supply of money would have no effect at all on the equilibrium level of national income, as shown in Figure 7.2. An increase in the supply of money from M_1 to M_2 shifts the LM curve from LM_1 to LM_2. But this has no effect on the equilibrium level of national income (Y_e). The only effect will be a fall in interest rates from r_1 to r_2.

Hence it is very important to consider whether or not a relationship exists between investment expenditure and the rate of interest, because if little or no relation exists then monetary policy will have no effect whatsoever on the equilibrium level of national income in conventional Keynesian macroeconomics. Most empirical studies do not include the market rate of interest as an explanatory variable in an investment equation. The reason is simply that variations in aggregate investment expenditure can be almost perfectly accounted for in terms of the accelerator model etc., as already illustrated.

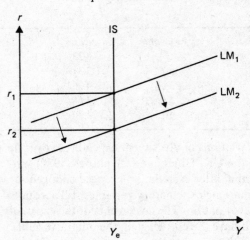

Figure 7.2

Investment and Interest Rates

The following aggregate investment equation for UK manufacturing industry was estimated by Hines and Catephores (1970) using quarterly data for the period 1956–67:

$$I_t = 15 \cdot 61 + 0 \cdot 691 I_{t-1} + 1 \cdot 696 \Delta Y_{t-3} + 1 \cdot 23 Y_{t-4}$$
$$(0 \cdot 084) \qquad (0 \cdot 734) \qquad (0 \cdot 282)$$
$$- 28 \cdot 822 \Delta R_{t-6} - 13 \cdot 559 R_{t-7}$$
$$(6 \cdot 193) \qquad (2 \cdot 887)$$

$$R^2 = 0 \cdot 944$$

where

I_t = gross fixed capital formation in manufacturing industry.
Y_t = index of output in manufacturing and is used as a proxy for demand.
R_t = quarterly average of the flat yield on $2 \cdot 5\%$ Consuls and is used as a proxy for the market rate of interest.
$\Delta Y_t = Y_t - Y_{t-1}$ etc.
$\Delta R_t = R_t - R_{t-1}$ etc.
t = time measured in quarters; hence $(t - K)$ indicates a lag of K quarters.

The value of the R^2 indicates that this equation can explain 94% of

Table 7.5

Variable	t-ratio
I_{t-1}	8·23
ΔY_{t-3}	2·31
Y_{t-4}	4·36
ΔR_{t-6}	4·65
R_{t-7}	4·70

quarterly variations in investment expenditure over the period 1956–67 in the UK. Hines and Catephores (1970) further discovered that after excluding the lagged endogenous variable I_{t-1} the remaining explanatory variables still accounted for over 70% of total variation. The coefficients of the explanatory variables all have the correct sign, the output variable being positive and the interest rate variable negative. The respective *t*-ratios are given in Table 7.5. In this case all the explanatory variables are significant at the 5% probability level, although ΔY_{t-3} is only just significant. The interesting point is that the two interest rate variables (ΔR and R) both perform quite well in terms of *t*-ratios and hence appear to have played a definite role in determining quarterly variations in UK investment expenditure.

Hines and Catephores concluded their study by pointing out that their results are consistent with a flexible version of the accelerator theory and that they are also consistent with the view that the long term rate of interest is an important determinant of investment in manufacturing industry. They also suggested that the failure of most econometric studies to discover a significant effect of the interest rate on investment was at least partially due to the use of annual data dominated by periods in which the interest rate was pegged. It appears that the IS curve is indeed downward-sloping and that monetary policy has some role to play in Keynesian macroeconomics. However Hines and Catephores pointed out that the elasticity of investment with respect to the rate of interest is less than the elasticity with respect to output, and furthermore that for investment expenditure the lags in monetary policy are greater than the lags in fiscal policy. This suggests a weak, but not totally ineffective, role for monetary policy in the Keynesian model.

Finally, let us consider some of the attempts by the National Institute of Economic and Social Research (NIESR) at estimating investment functions. In this case separate investment functions are estimated for manufacturing industries, the nationalised industries and the distributive trades respectively. Byron (1970) gave the following investment functions estimated by OLS and using UK quarterly data from 1959(3) to 1967(4), a total of 34 observations:

$$I_{man_t} = -198.92 + 0.0076 O_{man_{t-1}} + 0.0144 \Delta O_{man_t}$$
$$(0.007) \qquad (0.0282)$$

$$+ 1.894 SC_{man_{t-1}} + 0.216 TP_{t-1} + 0.509 I_{man_{t-1}}$$
$$(1.818) \qquad (0.132) \qquad (0.169)$$
$$R^2 = 0.57 \qquad DW = 2.20$$

$$I_{nat_t} = -105.14 + 0.057 O_{nat_{t-1}} + 0.0005 \Delta O_{nat_t} + 0.708 I_{nat_{t-1}}$$
$$(0.021) \qquad (0.0039) \qquad (0.116)$$
$$R^2 = 0.92 \qquad DW = 2.36$$

$$I_{dis_t} = 4.008 + 0.0050 O_{dis_{t-1}} + 0.0109 \Delta O_{dis_t} + 0.787 I_{dis_{t-1}}$$
$$(0.006) \qquad (0.029) \qquad (0.111)$$
$$R^2 = 0.81 \qquad DW = 2.36$$

where

I_{man} = gross fixed capital formation in manufacturing industries.
I_{nat} = gross fixed capital formation in nationalised industries.
I_{dis} = gross fixed capital formation in distributive trades.
O_{man} = output in manufacturing industries.
O_{nat} = output in nationalised industries.
O_{dis} = output in distributive trades.
SC_{man} = spare capacity in manufacturing industries.
TP = trading profits.

(The DW statistics indicate that all three tests were inconclusive at the 5% probability level.)

The first equation for the manufacturing industries is rather poor in terms of performance with only 57% of quarterly variation in investment expenditure explained. Furthermore, the lagged endogenous variable ($I_{man_{t-1}}$) is the only significant variable at the 5% probability level (and it would be very surprising if investment was not in some manner related to its value in the previous quarter!). Comparing this result directly with the study by Hines and Catephores, it appears that the lagged output term should be lagged four quarters rather than one and also that interest rates should be introduced if the explanatory power of this equation is to be improved over this period.

The second equation performs considerably better in terms of

R^2 with 92% of total variation in investment expenditure of the nationalised industries accounted for. The variables $O_{\text{nat}_{t-1}}$ and $I_{\text{nat}_{t-1}}$ were both significant at the 5% probability level with t-ratios of 2·714 and 6·103 respectively. Although in terms of R^2 the third equation for the distributive trades also performs well, the only significant variable is the lagged endogenous variable ($I_{\text{dis}_{t-1}}$) with a t-ratio of 7·09. Hence the improved fit in the second and third equations is due mainly to the fact that investment expenditure is more closely related to its value in the previous quarter in the nationalised industries and the distributive trades.

THE CONSUMPTION FUNCTION

Models of Consumption

Historically the notion of a consumption function began with the *absolute income hypothesis* of Keynes (1936). The consumption function was thought to possess the following characteristics:

1 A positive intercept on the consumption (C) axis.
2 A positive slope that is less than 1.
3 Average propensity to consume (APC) greater than marginal propensity to consume (MPC).
4 APC and MPC both diminishing as income (Y) increases.

These conditions yield the consumption function diagram shown in Figure 7.3.

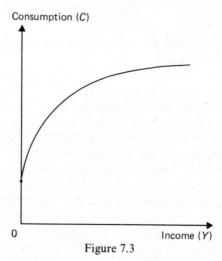

Figure 7.3

The absolute income hypothesis forecasted rather poorly. Just after the 1939–45 war it was discovered that, using cross-section data on household income, although the cross-section consumption function had a positive intercept and although APC > MPC the intercept shifted upwards over time. Initial attempts to incorporate this phenomenon included time as a separate explanatory variable into the consumption function, so that consumption would increase at any level of household income over time. The slope of the cross-section consumption function was estimated to be approximately 0·75 using interwar data. Kuznets (1942) had earlier shown using aggregate time-series data for the period 1869–1929 that the time-series consumption function was approximately a straight line through the origin, with MPC = APC = 0·9.

So a distinction was demonstrated between the time-series and cross-section consumption functions, as shown in Figures 7.4 and 7.5. The Keynesian absolute income hypothesis was consequently discredited, and subsequent research has attempted to reformulate the consumption function to reconcile the apparent inconsistency.

Probably the two most important attempts in this field were made by Ando and Modigliani (1963) with their *life cycle hypothesis* of consumer behaviour and by Friedman (1957) with his *permanent income hypothesis*. Both theories offer similar justifications for the observed discrepancy between the estimated MPCs from time-series and cross-section data. The life cycle hypothesis postulates that an individual's consumption is a function of his lifetime resources, which include his wealth, his current income and the discounted present value of his future earnings. The permanent income hypothesis divides income into a permanent and a transitory component, where transitory income consists of unanticipated windfall gains and losses; in this model an individual's consumption is proportional to his wealth, where wealth is discounted permanent income.

In both theories, if consumption is proportional to an individual's resources or permanent income a constant APC will be obtained over time. That is, the long-run consumption function for an individual will be a straight line passing through the origin. However, in cross-section data individual households are grouped by current income rather than by permanent income. On average, households with high current income have positive transitory

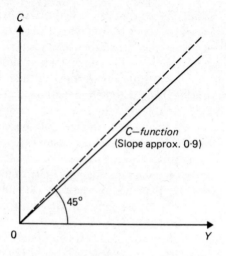

Figure 7.4

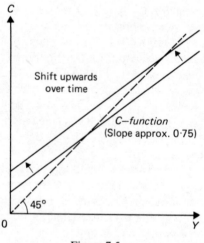

Figure 7.5

income since they have experienced temporary windfall gains, and households with low current income have experienced temporary windfall losses and therefore have negative transitory income. Hence the cross-section consumption function (Figure 7.5) will have a flatter slope (lower MPC) than the time-series consumption function (Figure 7.4), since households are basing their consumer spending on longer run notions of income or resources.

The rationale behind Friedman's (1957) model is illustrated in Figure 7.6. Let us denote permanent income by Y_p to distinguish it from current income (Y). Consider the typical household, represented by point A on the diagram. Their current income is Y_0, but their permanent income is less than this and equals Y_1. It is their permanent income on which they are basing their consumer spending (C_0). They have positive transitory income, and plotting measured income against consumer spending gives a

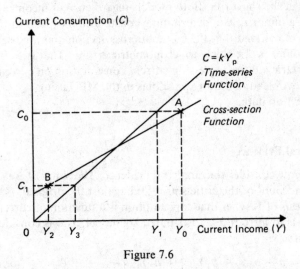

Figure 7.6

point such as A on the cross-section consumption function. On the other hand, consider the typical household at point B on the diagram. Their current income is Y_2, but their permanent income is greater than this and equals Y_3. It is this higher permanent income on which they are basing their consumer spending (C_1). In this case they have negative transitory income, and plotting measured income against consumer spending gives a point such as B on the cross-section consumption function.

Hence the cross-section consumption function passes through points A and B as depicted in Figure 7.6. However, when aggregating over all households to obtain aggregate time-series data Friedman assumed that transitory income averages out to zero and hence that measured income and permanent income become synonymous. Thus the long-run time-series consumption function is proportional to permanent income, as illustrated in the diagram, i.e.

$$C = kY_p$$

where k is a constant.

Both the life cycle and permanent income hypotheses explain the inconsistency between time-series and cross-section results by introducing into the analysis the unanticipated variability of income in the short run. Both models regard current income as playing a minor role in determining consumption expenditure. Friedman believed that the fact that cross-section and time-series results differ is due solely to 'econometric errors'. That is, econometric studies regressing current consumption on current income will lead to a downward bias in the MPC using cross-section data.

Empirical Evidence

Let us now consider the empirical evidence. The simplest way of taking account of the criticisms raised against the original hypothesis of Keynes that consumption is a function of current income is to introduce a distributed lag model, as was considered in chapter 6:

$$C_t = a + b_0 Y_t + b_1 Y_{t-1} + b_2 Y_{t-2} + \cdots + U_t$$

Assigning a series of geometrically declining weights to income in past time periods gave a consumption function of the form

$$C_t = a_1 + bY_t + cC_{t-1} + U_{1t}$$

In other words, C_t is regressed on Y_t and C_{t-1}. Evans (1969, chapter 3) estimated the following annual time-series consumption function using US data over the period 1929–62, excluding war years:

$$C_t = 0{\cdot}28 Y_t + 0{\cdot}676 C_{t-1}$$
$$\quad (0{\cdot}041) \quad (0{\cdot}052)$$

$$R^2 = 0{\cdot}998 \qquad DW = 1{\cdot}09$$

This is as close to a perfect fit as one can get, with 99·8% of total variation in consumers' expenditure accounted for. But recall from chapter 6 that the OLS method will yield a biased estimate of the coefficient of a lagged endogenous variable when the error term is autocorrelated. The very low value of the DW statistic is clear evidence of positive serial correlation at the 5% probability level, and hence the estimated coefficient of C_{t-1}, i.e. 0·676, is almost certainly biased.

Most of the empirical work on the life cycle hypothesis by Ando and Modigliani (1963) used time-series data for the USA over the period 1929–59, excluding the war years 1941–6. They included several different variables into the consumption function but discovered that the most successful explanatory variables were current income (Y_t) and wealth (or net worth) in the previous year (W_{t-1}). The result of this regression was

$$C_t = 0·56Y_t + 0·081W_{t-1}$$
$$(0·09) \quad (0·015)$$

$$R^2 = 0·997 \qquad DW = 0·33$$

Unfortunately, as can be seen from the extremely low value of the DW statistic, this procedure resulted in extremely high positive serial correlation. The autocorrelation was so high that the reliability of the estimates were, in the opinion of Ando and Modigliani, open to serious question.

It was pointed out in chapter 5 that a common procedure in time-series analysis when the serial correlation of the error terms is high is to work with first differences. Ando and Modigliani accordingly adopted this approach and obtained the following estimated equation:

$$\Delta C_t = 0·52\Delta Y_t + 0·072\Delta W_{t-1}$$
$$(0·11) \quad (0·018)$$

$$R^2 = 0·929 \qquad DW = 1·85$$

Ando and Modigliani considered this result to be quite favourable to the life cycle hypothesis. The R^2 is very high, and the coefficient of net worth is clearly significant at the 5% probability level with a t-ratio of 4·0. Also the DW statistic improves considerably, showing no autocorrelation at the 5% probability level.
However, the t-ratios are rather disappointing (4·73 and 4·0 for ΔY_t and ΔW_{t-1} respectively) due to the relatively high estimated

standard errors. It is clear that very reliable estimates of the role of each of the explanatory variables cannot be obtained.

Hilton and Crossfield (1970, appendix B) tested the following consumption function:

$$C_t = b_1 W_t + b_2 Y_t + b_3 \Delta Y_t + b_4 \Delta G_t + b_5 C_{t-1}$$

where

Y = personal disposable income in a quarter.
W = personal sector wealth at the beginning of that quarter.
C = consumers' expenditure.
t = time measured in quarters.
G = a variable indicating hire-purchase restrictions.

This equation was estimated using UK quarterly data for the period 1955(2)–65(4). The results using the OLS method of estimation are given in Table 7.6. Once again the estimated

Table 7.6

Coefficient	Estimated value	t-ratio
b_1	0·018	2·0
b_2	0·218	2·1
b_3	0·410	3·3
b_4	−1·250	2·1
b_5	0·579	4·1

$R^2 = 0.9953$ $DW = 2.28$

equation fits the data almost perfectly, indicating that 99·53% of total variation in consumers' expenditure can be accounted for. However, the t-ratios are fairly low, with the coefficients of wealth, current disposable income and the change in hire-purchase terms just barely significant at the 5% probability level. It is impossible to obtain very reliable estimates of the role of each of the explanatory variables. The DW statistic indicates that the test was inconclusive at the 5% probability level.

Chapter 8

Structural Equations and the Identification Problem

SUPPLY AND DEMAND CURVES

Let us return to the problem of estimating the demand and supply curves of some commodity, e.g. wine, from actual observations on price and quantity over a specified period of time. In general it might be assumed that:

1 Quantity demanded (Q_d) is a function of price of wine, price of substitutes and complements, and disposable income.
2 Quantity supplied (Q_s) is a function of price of wine, price of other agricultural commodities, costs of production, temperature and rainfall.

The construction of demand and supply curves is an attempt to analyse the effect on Q_d and Q_s of a change in the price of wine (P), assuming that all other variables entering the demand and supply functions remain constant. But clearly these exogenous variables will change over the course of time, and the demand and supply curves will shift accordingly. Let us take 52 weekly observations on the quantity of wine consumed and the market price. Thus in any particular week the equilibrium price and quantity are observed, given specific values for all the exogenous variables.

If price and quantity are observed weekly during any month, the demand and supply curves will both be found to have shifted due to changes in the exogenous variables, as illustrated, for example, in Figure 8.1. The price and quantity combinations (P_1, Q_1), (P_2, Q_2), (P_3, Q_3) and (P_4, Q_4) are all observed, but fitting a line

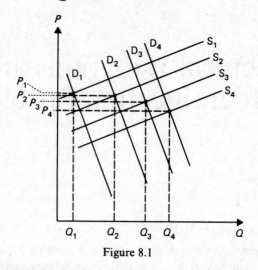

Figure 8.1

through these observations yields neither the true demand curve nor the true supply curve.

Extending this to 52 weekly observations on price and quantity, it is quite probable that a fairly random scatter of points will be obtained when these are plotted on the price–quantity axes, as illustrated in Figure 8.2. Such a cluster of points can be produced equally well by any pair of lines intersecting, and it is clearly

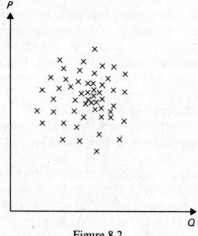

Figure 8.2

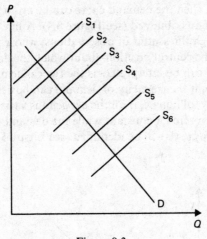

Figure 8.3

impossible to obtain any knowledge about the shape of the demand or supply curve from the plot.

Of course, if all the exogenous variables in the demand equation remain fixed over the time period considered while the supply curve shifts, then the demand curve may be identified from the scatter of observations (see Figure 8.3). More realistically, if the shifts in the supply curve are far greater than the shifts in the

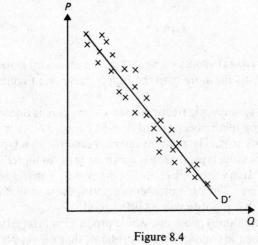

Figure 8.4

demand curve, then the demand curve can be estimated from the set of observations obtained (see Figure 8.4). A line such as D′ can be fitted through the scatter of observations, whose position will approximate the central position about which the demand curve has shifted. D′ can be interpreted as the typical demand curve for wine, and from it the elasticity of demand can be determined.

Alternatively, of course, if all the exogenous variables in the supply equation remain constant while the demand curve shifts, then the supply curve will be identified (see Figure 8.5). Or, more

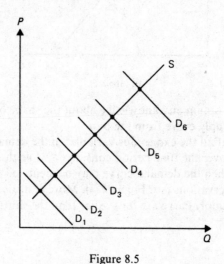

Figure 8.5

realistically, the typical supply curve (S′) can be estimated if the demand curve shifts far more than the supply curve (see Figure 8.6).

This simple diagrammatic treatment shows that care is needed in interpreting any relationship found to exist between market price and quantity sold. The relationship may identify (a) a typical demand curve, or (b) a typical supply curve, or (c) a 'mongrel' relationship that in no way reflects either the typical demand or typical supply curve. For example, Moore (1914) thought that he had determined that pig-iron was a Giffen good!

With most agricultural products, where production is largely influenced by climatic conditions, it is probable that the supply

curve will shift far more than the demand curve, which implies
that the typical demand curve will be identified. Furthermore, it is
possible to correct the data so as to remove the effects of some of
the exogenous variables in the demand equation. For example,
adjustment is usually made for changes in the purchasing power of
money by dividing all the original price data by an index of the
general level of prices.

Hence whether or not the demand curve or the supply curve is
identified from fitting a curve through a series of points depends
not only on the fundamental nature of demand and supply

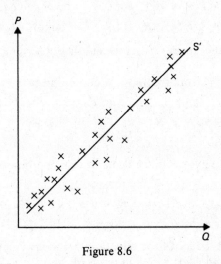

Figure 8.6

conditions but also on the nature of the corrections applied to the
original data. By applying suitable corrections to the data it may
be possible to estimate the demand curve even though the original
demand curve fluctuated just as much as the supply curve.

Under certain circumstances it may be possible to estimate both
the demand curve and the supply curve from the original data on
price and quantity sold in the market. Let us first consider the
identification problem in greater depth.

REDUCED-FORM EQUATIONS

So far only *structural relationships* have been considered. That is,
each equation in the model represents a specific economic

relationship, i.e. the demand and supply equations. However, any such set of structural equations can be solved for each of the endogenous variables in terms of the exogenous variables only, to give *reduced-form equations*.

In our model of the wine market let us consider *a priori* that the two most important variables in the demand equation are price (P) and per capita income (Y), and that the two most important variables in the supply equation are price (P) and rainfall (R). Then the demand and supply equations can be written as follows, assuming they are approximately linear in form:

$$Q_t = a_1 + b_1 P_t + d_1 Y_t + U_{1t} \qquad \text{demand equation}$$
$$Q_t = a_2 + b_2 P_t + c_2 R_t + U_{2t} \qquad \text{supply equation}$$

where U_1 and U_2 are error terms and the subscript t denotes the time period.

Eliminating Q from the above equations gives the reduced form for P:

$$P_t = \frac{a_2 - a_1 + c_2 R_t - d_1 Y_t + U_{2t} - U_{1t}}{b_1 - b_2}$$

and substituting for P in the demand equation gives the reduced form for Q:

$$Q_t = \frac{b_1 a_2 - b_2 a_1 + b_1 c_2 R_t - b_2 d_1 Y_t + b_1 U_{2t} - b_2 U_{1t}}{b_1 - b_2}$$

These are the reduced-form equations for the two endogenous variables P and Q expressed in terms of the exogenous variables and error terms only. For simplicity, they can be rewritten as

$$P_t = f_1 + g_1 R_t + h_1 Y_t + V_{1t} \qquad (1)$$
$$Q_t = f_2 + g_2 R_t + h_2 Y_t + V_{2t} \qquad (2)$$

where

$$f_1 = (a_2 - a_1)/(b_1 - b_2) \qquad f_2 = (b_1 a_2 - b_2 a_1)/(b_1 - b_2)$$
$$g_1 = c_2/(b_1 - b_2) \qquad g_2 = b_1 c_2/(b_1 - b_2)$$
$$h_1 = -d_1/(b_1 - b_2) \qquad h_2 = -b_2 d_1/(b_1 - b_2)$$
$$V_{1t} = (U_{2t} - U_{1t})/(b_1 - b_2) \quad V_{2t} = (b_1 U_{2t} - b_2 U_{1t})/(b_1 - b_2)$$

Now each of the reduced-form equations 1 and 2 above can be estimated by the OLS method to obtain estimates of the parameters

f_1, f_2, g_1, g_2, h_1 and h_2. Let us denote these estimates by $\hat{f}_1, \hat{f}_2, \hat{g}_1,$ $\hat{g}_2, \hat{h}_1$ and $\hat{h}_2$ respectively. Then the values obtained for these estimates can be used to derive in turn estimates of the parameters in the structural equations, by solving the following set of equations:

$$\hat{f}_1 = (a_2 - a_1)/(b_1 - b_2) \qquad \hat{f}_2 = (b_1 a_2 - b_2 a_1)/(b_1 - b_2)$$
$$\hat{g}_1 = c_2/(b_1 - b_2) \qquad\qquad \hat{g}_2 = b_1 c_2/(b_1 - b_2)$$
$$\hat{h}_1 = -d_1/(b_1 - b_2) \qquad\quad \hat{h}_2 = -b_2 d_1/(b_1 - b_2)$$

The important point is that there are six equations with six unknowns, i.e. a_1, a_2, b_1, b_2, c_2 and d_1, given the obtained estimates of the reduced-form coefficients. Thus these equations can be solved to obtain estimates of all the coefficients in both the demand and supply equations. Denoting these estimates by $\hat{a}_1, \hat{a}_2,$ $\hat{b}_1, \hat{b}_2, \hat{c}_2$ and $\hat{d}_1$, the following estimated demand and supply equations are obtained:

$$\hat{Q}_t = \hat{a}_1 + \hat{b}_1 P_t + \hat{d}_1 Y_t \qquad \text{estimated demand equation}$$
$$\hat{Q}_t = \hat{a}_2 + \hat{b}_2 P_t + \hat{c}_2 R_t \qquad \text{estimated supply equation}$$

Therefore it has been shown in this case that it is possible to estimate both the supply and demand functions from the original data on price and quantity sold in the market. In other words, the demand equation and the supply equation are both *identified*. The crux of the identification problem is whether or not unique values can be obtained for all the coefficients in the structural equations from the estimated reduced-form equations. In the above example this was indeed possible because there were six equations involving six unknowns, which enabled unique estimates of the structural coefficients to be obtained.

Consider another example where this time it is believed that climatic conditions play an important role in both the demand and supply equations for, say, strawberries. Suppose that temperature (T) is considered to have an important influence on both the demand and supply of strawberries in addition to price (P). Again assuming a linear relationship:

$$Q_t = a_1 + b_1 P_t + c_1 T_t + U_{1t} \qquad \text{demand equation}$$
$$Q_t = a_2 + b_2 P_t + c_2 T_t + U_{2t} \qquad \text{supply equation}$$

The reduced form equations for P and Q are given by

$$P_t = f_1 + g_1 T_t + V_{1t}$$
$$Q_t = f_2 + g_2 T_t + V_{2t}$$

where

$$f_1 = (a_2 - a_1)/(b_1 - b_2) \qquad f_2 = (b_1 a_2 - b_2 a_1)/(b_1 - b_2)$$
$$g_1 = (c_2 - c_1)/(b_1 - b_2) \qquad g_2 = (b_1 c_2 - b_2 c_1)/(b_1 - b_2)$$
$$V_{1t} = (U_{2t} - U_{1t})/(b_1 - b_2) \quad V_{2t} = (b_1 U_{2t} - b_2 U_{1t})/(b_1 - b_2)$$

However, if the OLS method is used to obtain estimates of the reduced-form parameters, i.e. $\hat{f}_1, \hat{f}_2, \hat{g}_1$ and $\hat{g}_2$, and it is then attempted to derive estimates of the structural equations, it is clear that there will be six unknowns in only four equations, i.e.

$$\hat{f}_1 = (a_2 - a_1)/(b_1 - b_2) \qquad \hat{f}_2 = (b_1 a_2 - b_2 a_1)/(b_1 - b_2)$$
$$\hat{g}_1 = (c_2 - c_1)/(b_1 - b_2) \qquad \hat{g}_2 = (b_1 c_2 - b_2 c_1)/(b_1 - b_2)$$

Clearly, unique values of the structural parameters $a_1, a_2, b_1, b_2,$ c_1 and c_2 cannot be obtained from the above equations. In this example neither the demand equation nor the supply equation can be identified. There are an infinite series of values of $a_1, a_2, b_1, b_2,$ c_1 and c_2 that will give rise to the same values of $\hat{f}_1, \hat{f}_2, \hat{g}_1$ and $\hat{g}_2$ and hence to the same reduced form.

It is apparent that the identification problem is directly linked to the number of distinct exogenous variables included in the structural equations. Thus in the first example there was a distinct exogenous variable included in each of the structural equations, i.e. per capita income (Y) in the demand equation and rainfall (R) in the supply equation. This ensured that there would be an equal number of equations and unknowns and hence in theory made it possible to identify both the demand and supply equations. In the second example, however, the same exogenous variable (T) was present in each of the structural relationships, which did not enable sufficient information to be acquired from the reduced-form equations to identify either the demand or the supply equation.

Of course, the reduced-form equations can always be estimated even if the structural relations cannot be identified. But clearly this is cold comfort to economists, as they are interested in the economic structure *per se*, e.g. demand and supply equations.

Exercise 8.1

1 Explain what you understand by the terms 'structural equation' and 'reduced-form equation'.

2 What is meant by saying that a structural equation cannot be identified?

3 A demand and supply model has two endogenous variables, P and Q, and two exogenous variables, Y and R. Both relationships are assumed to be linear, and the only other restriction is that Y does not enter the supply relation. Find the reduced-form equations for the two structures below, and state whether either or both relationships are identified.

$$Q_t = -2P_t + R_t + 3Y_t + U_{1t} \qquad \text{demand A}$$
$$Q_t = P_t + 2R_t + U_{2t} \qquad \text{supply A}$$
$$Q_t = -P_t + \tfrac{4}{3}R_t + 2Y_t + U_{1t} \qquad \text{demand B}$$
$$Q_t = P_t + 2R_t + U_{2t} \qquad \text{supply B}$$

4 Will the identification of models A and B above be affected if from a particular set of data:
(a) R has a constant value?
(b) Y has a constant value?

TWO-STAGE LEAST SQUARES METHOD OF ESTIMATION

Let us now consider the problem of estimation, taking our wine market example where both the demand and supply curves were identifiable, i.e.

$$Q_t = a_1 + b_1 P_t + d_1 Y_t + U_{1t} \qquad \text{demand equation}$$
$$Q_t = a_2 + b_2 P_t + c_2 R_t + U_{2t} \qquad \text{supply equation}$$

Estimation of the demand equation by the OLS method will result in a biased estimate of the coefficient b_1, and in the case of the supply equation it will result in a biased estimate of the coefficient b_2. The reason for this can best be explained by considering the reduced-form equation for P:

$$P_t = \frac{a_2 - a_1 + c_2 R_t - d_1 Y_t + U_{2t} - U_{1t}}{b_1 - b_2}$$

From the error term it can be seen that P_t is related to both U_{1t} and U_{2t}, the error terms in each of the structural equations. Hence the standard assumptions for obtaining unbiased estimates of the coefficients b_1 and b_2 using the OLS method of estimation are not satisfied, since P_t is not independent of the error terms in the demand and supply equations. Better estimates of the parameters can be obtained by using an alternative method of estimation known as two-stage least squares (TSLS). The estimates of b_1 and b_2 obtained from the TSLS method of estimation give *consistent* estimates of b_1 and b_2. As explained in chapter 2, this means that the bias disappears as the sample size becomes very large, so that the bias will still be present in small samples.

The TSLS method makes use of the reduced-form equation for P to obtain estimates of the structural equations. Let us write the reduced-form equation for P as

$$P_t = f_1 + g_1 R_t + h_1 Y_t + V_{1t}$$

If the exact form of this equation was known, i.e. if the true values of f_1, g_1, h_1 and V_{1t} were known (for all values of t), then indeed *unbiased* estimates of all the coefficients in the structural equations could be obtained, since the error term

$$V_{1t} = (U_{2t} - U_{1t})/(b_1 - b_2)$$

could be removed from this equation and P could be replaced by P^*, where

$$P_t^* = f_1 + g_1 R_t + h_1 Y_t$$

An OLS regression of Q on P^* and Y, and of Q on P^* and R, would yield unbiased estimates of the coefficients in the demand and supply equations respectively, since P_t^* is unrelated to both U_{1t} and U_{2t}.

In practice the actual values of f_1, g_1 and h_1 are not known, but of course these values can be estimated by means of an OLS regression of P on R and Y, giving $\hat{f}_1, \hat{g}_1$ and $\hat{h}_1$. Then the known residual element can be removed from this regression, giving

$$\hat{P}_t = \hat{f}_1 + \hat{g}_1 R_t + \hat{h}_1 Y_t$$

for all values of t. Using $\hat{P}$ as a proxy variable for the unknown P^*, now P is replaced by $\hat{P}$ in both the demand and supply equations. It can be shown that an OLS regression of Q on $\hat{P}$ and

Y, and of Q on $\hat{P}$ and R, would give consistent estimates of b_1 and b_2.

This is the two-stage least squares method of estimation, so named because (a) in the first stage an OLS regression of the reduced-form equation is done to calculate $\hat{P}$, and (b) in the second stage P is replaced by $\hat{P}$ in the structural equations and an OLS regression of Q on $\hat{P}$ and Y, and of Q on $\hat{P}$ and R, is done to obtain estimates of the structural parameters. Hence there are two stages involved in the TSLS procedure, each involving the OLS method of estimation.

Simultaneity Problem

The problems involved in estimating simultaneous equation systems are clearly complex. In the first place it must be ensured that the individual equations can be identified. (Otherwise, for example, it may be believed that a Giffen good has been discovered instead of a conventional upward-sloping supply curve!) Secondly, an appropriate method of estimation has to be chosen, bearing in mind that OLS will give biased and inconsistent estimates.

Thus far only demand and supply equations have been considered. However, the estimation of simultaneous equations arises, for example, in several of the macroeconomic case studies considered in the previous chapter. In the study of wage and price inflation the rate of change of the retail price index (ΔP) has been an important determinant in trade union wage demands and hence has directly affected the rate of change of money wage rates (ΔW). In turn, of course, wage rates are an important element in a firm's costs and hence directly affect prices. Thus ΔW and ΔP are both endogenous variables, and there exists a simultaneous system of equations in a wage–price model. OLS estimation of the wage equation will result in a biased estimate of the coefficient of ΔP; similarly OLS estimation of the price equation will result in a biased estimate of the coefficient of ΔW.

This simultaneity problem also arises in the estimation of consumption functions using data on aggregate consumers' expenditure and national income, because not only is Y an important determinant of the level of C, but also C is itself an important element in determining the level of Y. Hence Y is an endogenous variable and will not be independent of the error term in a consumption function. OLS estimation of a consumption function will give a biased estimate of the coefficient of Y.

Again the simultaneity problem arises in the field of monetary policy and its efficacy. Monetarists believe that the stock of money (M) directly influences the level of national income (Y), and they have attempted to illustrate the efficacy of monetary policy by means of regressing Y upon M (or ΔY upon ΔM). But if the reasonable presumption is accepted that the central authorities vary the supply of money to meet demand in response to changes in national income, then it follows that, if both theories are correct, M will be an endogenous variable in any regression of Y upon M. Hence M will not be independent of the error term, with the result that OLS estimation will give a biased estimate of the coefficient of M.

Exercise 8.2

The data in Table 8.1 is assumed to be generated by the following demand–supply model:

$$Q_t = a_1 + b_1 P_t + U_{1t} \qquad \text{supply equation}$$
$$Q_t = a_2 + b_2 P_t + c_2 A_t + U_{2t} \qquad \text{demand equation}$$

Quantity (Q) and price (P) are endogenous variables, index of

Table 8.1

t	Q	P	A
1	36	33	5
2	81	78	15
3	47	48	11
4	84	71	10
5	71	56	8
6	61	48	8
7	51	50	8
8	61	60	12
9	76	61	9
10	61	48	6
11	23	28	6
12	76	67	12

$\hat{a}_1 = -3\cdot93 \qquad \hat{b}_1 = 1\cdot20 \qquad \hat{f}_1 = 16\cdot25 \qquad \hat{g}_1 = 4\cdot12$

advertising expenditure (A) is treated as exogenous, and U_1 and U_2 are error terms.

The OLS estimate of the supply equation is

$$\hat{Q}_t = \hat{a}_1 + \hat{b}_1 P_t$$

and the OLS estimate of the reduced-form equation for P_t is

$$\hat{P}_t = \hat{f}_1 + \hat{g}_1 A_t$$

1 Discuss the identification of the model.
2 Obtain the two-stage least squares estimate of the supply equation by regressing Q_t on $\hat{P}_t$, and compare it with the ordinary least squares estimate.

COMPARISON OF THE TSLS AND OLS METHODS

In spite of the obvious advantage of the TSLS over the OLS method when dealing with simultaneous equations, i.e. the removal of the OLS inconsistency, the OLS method still has certain advantages. First, the TSLS method does not yield as accurate an R^2 as the OLS method, and for this reason empirical studies using the TSLS procedure often omit the R^2. On more than one occasion when employing the TSLS method of estimation I have obtained an R^2 greater than 1! Secondly, the OLS method is the best to use for the purpose of prediction. Suppose, for example, that the government, having negotiated with the trade unions to determine the rate of wage inflation for the forthcoming year, wishes to predict what the rate of price inflation will be. The OLS method of estimation will give the government the best prediction. Walters (1970) summarised the various properties of these two methods very concisely in the manner given in Table 8.2.

Table 8.2

Purpose	*OLS*	*TSLS*
To estimate structural parameters	Biased and inconsistent	Consistent (although biased in small samples)
To predict an endogenous variable	Unbiased and best	Biased and inefficient

The various tests and statistics employed for the purpose of analysing econometric results were designed for the use of the OLS method and do not possess the same properties when other methods of estimation are used. For this reason many studies involved with the estimation of simultaneous equation systems publish the results from using both OLS and TSLS methods. More sophisticated methods for estimating simultaneous equation models also exist, such as the three-stage least squares (3SLS), limited-information maximum-likelihood (LIML), and full-information maximum-likelihood (FIML) methods. However, these methods are rarely used except in a few large econometric models of the entire economy, and their consideration is beyond the scope of this book.

Finally, let us consider the differences in the estimates obtained by the two methods of OLS and TSLS. First, let us return to the topic of wage and price inflation where clearly there exists a simultaneous system of equations, as explained previously.

Hines's Study of Unionisation and Wage Inflation

Hines (1964), in his study of trade unions and wage inflation in the UK during the period 1921–61 (excluding war years), estimated the following set of equations:

wage equation

$$\Delta W_t = a_1 + b_1 \Delta T_t + c_1 T_t + d_1 \Delta P_t + e_1 \Delta P_{t-1} + f_1 U_t$$

price equation

$$\Delta P_t = a_2 + b_2 \Delta W_t + c_2 \Delta M_{t-\frac{1}{2}} + d_2 \Delta X_t$$

unionisation equation

$$\Delta T_t = a_3 + b_3 T_{t-1} + c_3 \Delta P_t + d_3 \Delta P_{t-1} + e_3 D_{t-\frac{1}{2}}$$

Thus he proposed three structural equations and three endogenous variables, i.e. ΔW_t, ΔP_t and ΔT_t, where:

ΔW = % rate of change of an index of money wage rates.
T = % of labour force unionised.
ΔT = rate of change of % of labour force unionised.
U = % of labour force unemployed.
ΔP = % rate of change of the retail price index.

$\Delta M = \%$ rate of change of an index of import prices.

$\Delta X = \%$ rate of change of an index of productivity per man year.

$D =$ level of money profits deflated by the index of retail prices.

The results from using OLS and TSLS estimation methods are given in Table 8.3.

Table 8.3

	Wage equation			Price equation			Unionisation equation	
	OLS	TSLS		OLS	TSLS		OLS	TSLS
$a_1 =$	0·7445	−1·9740	$a_2 =$	−0·2344	0·7797	$a_3 =$	1·7109	1·4014
$b_1 =$	1·5114	1·5945	$b_2 =$	0·5857	0·6924	$b_3 =$	−0·1131	−0·1145
	(2·95)[a]	(6·59)		(7·14)	(19·9)		(5·19)	(13·8)
$c_1 =$	0·0639	0·1282	$c_2 =$	0·0844	0·0396	$c_3 =$	0·4265	0·4664
	(0·43)	(3·13)		(1·91)	(2·29)		(11·7)	(31·5)
$d_1 =$	0·6199	0·6804	$d_2 =$	−0·0042	0·1346	$d_3 =$	−0·0680	−0·0978
	(2·66)	(6·03)		(0·02)	(1·86)[b]		(1·62)[b]	(7·58)[b]
$e_1 =$	−0·0409	−0·0812				$e_3 =$	0·0118	0·0149
	(0·39)[b]	(2·94)[b]					(0·93)	(3·10)
$f_1 =$	−0·1243	−0·0441						
	(0·79)	(1·19)						
$R^2 =$	0·9141	0·9953	$R^2 =$	0·8963	0·9834	$R^2 =$	0·8762	0·9843

[a] Figures in parentheses are *t*-ratios.
[b] The coefficient has the wrong sign.

The only important explanatory variables in the wage equation were ΔT_t and ΔP_t, and their coefficients (i.e. b_1 and d_1 respectively) are a little higher when estimated by TSLS as opposed to OLS. In the price equation the only important explanatory variable was ΔW_t, and its coefficient (i.e. b_2) is significantly higher when estimated by TSLS as opposed to OLS. In the unionisation equation the only important explanatory variables were ΔP_t and T_{t-1}; the coefficient of T_{t-1} (i.e. b_3) is approximately the same in both cases, but the coefficient of ΔP_t (i.e. c_3) is a little higher when estimated by TSLS as opposed to OLS. The extremely high values of the R^2 in all three equations when TSLS is used must be interpreted with caution in view of their possible inaccuracy. To summarise, the results indicate that the OLS method of estimation gave estimates of the coefficients b_1, d_1, b_2 and c_3 that were biased downwards.

Klein Model I

Secondly, let us consider a very simple macroeconomic model of the economy. Klein (1950) produced the following simple model (Klein Model I):

$$C_t = a_0 + a_1 P_t + a_2 P_{t-1} + a_3(W_1 + W_2)_t + U_{1t}$$
$$I_t = b_0 + b_1 P_t + b_2 P_{t-1} + b_3 K_{t-1} + U_{2t}$$
$$W_{1t} = c_0 + c_1(Y + T - W_2)_t + c_2(Y + T - W_2)_{t-1}$$
$$+ c_3(t - 1931) + U_{3t}$$

$$Y \equiv C + I + G - T$$
$$Y \equiv P + W_1 + W_2$$
$$I_t \equiv K_t - K_{t-1}$$

where

C = consumers' expenditure.
P = profits.
W_1 = wage bill for the private sector.
W_2 = wage bill for the government sector.
I = investment expenditure.
Y = net national product in the economy.
T = business taxes.
K = capital stock.
G = government expenditure.
t = a time trend.
U_1, U_2, U_3 = error terms.

In the first equation consumption is related to the two components of national income: profits and wages. The second equation embodies a profits model of investment expenditure. The third equation relates wages in the private sector (used as a proxy variable for employment) to an index of output in the private sector and a time trend. The first identity relates net national product to its component sum of total expenditure net of taxation. The second identity expresses national product as the sum of the component parts of income. The third, of course, expresses net investment as the rate of change of the capital stock.

This model is the polar opposite in size and detail to the Brookings model project, which was started in 1959 (see

Duesenberry, Fromm, Klein and Kuh, 1965). The Brookings model contains no less than 203 equations with detailed treatment of the investment, construction, financial, public and agricultural sectors of the US economy. There are over 200 exogenous variables included. The estimation of the Brookings model is mainly by the LIML method, but there is some use of TSLS and some OLS.

To return to the Klein model I, Desai (1976) analysed this model using US interwar data from 1921–41. In chapter 8 of his book he has provided alternative estimates of the Klein model I parameters using various methods of estimation. The results for OLS and TSLS are given in Table 8.4 (rounded to the nearest three significant figures):

Table 8.4

Consumption equation			Investment equation			Wage equation		
	OLS	TSLS		OLS	TSLS		OLS	TSLS
$a_0 =$	16·40	16·60	$b_0 =$	10·10	20·30	$c_0 =$	1·50	1·50
$a_1 =$	0·25	0·02	$b_1 =$	0·49	0·15	$c_1 =$	0·44	0·44
$a_2 =$	0·00	0·22	$b_2 =$	0·33	0·62	$c_2 =$	0·15	0·15
$a_3 =$	0·80	0·81	$b_3 =$	−0·11	−0·16	$c_3 =$	0·13	0·13

The OLS and the TSLS estimates of the third equation, the wage equation, are identical (as given by c_0, c_1, c_2 and c_3). In the first equation, the consumption function, the constant term (a_0) and the coefficient of the wage bill (a_3) have produced almost identical estimates, but a_1 and a_2 (the coefficients of current and lagged profits respectively) are significantly different using OLS and TSLS. In fact the relative importance of current and lagged profits are reversed when the different methods of estimation are compared, in the sense that the sum of a_1 and a_2 is approximately the same which ever method is used, but the OLS method attributes all the importance to a_1 whereas the TSLS method attributes almost all the importance to a_2. The OLS and the TSLS estimates of the second equation, the investment equation, differ rather more, although it is interesting to note that once again the relative importance of current and lagged profits as explanatory variables are reversed.

Exercise 8.3

1   Compare and contrast the method of ordinary least squares with the method of two-stage least squares.
2   Illustrate the differences in the two methods with reference to a particular economic case study you have read about in which both methods of estimation have been employed.

References

Aftalion, A. (1909) 'La réalité des surproductions générales, essui d'une théorie des crises générales et periodiques', *Revue d'Economic Politique*.

Amey, L. R. (1964) 'Diversified manufacturing businesses', *Journal of the Royal Statistical Society*, pt 2, vol. 127, ser. A (general).

Ando, A. and Modigliani, F. (1963) 'The "life cycle" hypothesis of saving: aggregate implications and tests', *American Economic Review*, vol. LIII, no. 1, pt 1 (March).

Byron, R. P. (1970) 'Initial attempts at econometric model building at NIESR', in K. Hilton and D. F. Heathfield (eds), *The Econometric Study of the United Kingdom* (London: Macmillan).

Chenery, H. B. (1952) 'Overcapacity and the acceleration principle', *Econometrica*, vol. 20, no. 1 (January).

Clark, J. M. (1917) 'Business acceleration and the law of demand', *Journal of Political Economy*, vol. 25, no. 1 (March).

Desai, M. (1975) 'The Phillips curve: a revisionist interpretation', *Economica*, vol. 42, nos 165–8.

Desai, M. (1976) *Applied Econometrics* (London: Philip Allan).

Duesenberry, J. S., Fromm, G., Klein, L. R. and Kuh, E. (eds) (1965) *The Brookings Quarterly Econometric Model of the United States Economy* (Chicago: Rand McNally).

Evans, M. K. (1969) *Macroeconomic Activity* (New York: Harper & Row).

Friedman, M. (1957) *A Theory of the Consumption Function* (Princeton, NJ: Princeton University Press).

Friedman, M. (1968) 'The role of monetary policy', *American Economic Review*, vol. LVIII, no. 1.

Goodwin, R. M. (1951) 'The non-linear accelerator and the persistence of business cycles', *Econometrica*, vol. 19, no. 1 (January).

Grunfeld, Y. (1960) 'The determinants of corporate investment', in A. C. Harberger (ed), *The Demand for Durable Goods* (Chicago: University of Chicago Press).

Hilton, K. and Crossfield, D. H. (1970) 'Short-run consumption functions for the UK, 1955–66', in K. Hilton and D. F. Heathfield (eds), *The Econometric Study of the United Kingdom* (London: Macmillan).

Hines, A. G. (1964) 'Trade unions and wage inflation in the United Kingdom 1893–1961', *Review of Economic Studies*, vol. 31.

Hines, A. G. and Catephores, G. (1970) 'Investment in UK manufacturing industry, 1956–67', in K. Hilton and D. F. Heathfield (eds), *The Econometric Study of the United Kingdom* (London: Macmillan).

Johnston, J. (1972) *Econometric Methods*, 2nd edn (New York: McGraw-Hill).

Kaldor, N. (1970) 'The new monetarism', *Lloyds Bank Review*, no. 97 (July).

Keynes, J. M. (1936) *The General Theory of Employment, Interest and Money* (New York: Harcourt Brace).

Klein, L. R. (1950) *Economic Fluctuations in the United States 1921–1941*, Cowles Commission Monograph 11 (New York: Wiley).

Kuznets, S. (1942) *Uses of National Income in Peace and War* (New York: National Bureau of Economic Research).

Lipsey, R. G. (1960) 'The relation between unemployment and the rate of change of money wage rates in the UK 1862–1957: a further study', *Economica*, vol. XXVII, nos 105–8.

Lund, P. (1971) *Investment: Study of an Economic Aggregate* (London: Oliver & Boyd).

Moore, H. (1914) *Economic Cycles: Their Law and Causes* (see article by E. J. Working, 'What do statistical "demand curves" show?', *Quarterly Journal of Economics*, vol. XLI, 1927).

Phillips, A. (1958) 'The relationship between unemployment and the rate of change of money wage rates in the UK 1861–1957', *Economica*, vol. XXV, nos 97–100.

Schumpeter, J. A. (1954) *History of Economic Analysis* (London: Allen & Unwin).

Solow, R. (1969) *Price Expectations and the Behaviour of the Price Level* (Manchester: Manchester University Press).

Surrey, M. J. C. (1971) *The Analysis and Forecasting of the British Economy* (London: NIESR).

Walters, A. A. (1970) *An Introduction to Econometrics*, 2nd edn (London: Macmillan).

Walters, A. A. (1971) *Money in Boom and Slump*, 3rd edn, Hobart Paper no. 44 (London: Institute of Economic Affairs).

Wynn, R. and Holden, K. (1974) *Introduction to Applied Econometric Analysis* (London: Macmillan).

Further Reading

ECONOMETRIC THEORY
R. J. Allard, *An Approach to Econometrics* (London: Philip Allan, 1974).
J. Johnston, *Econometric Methods*, 2nd edn (New York: McGraw-Hill, 1972).
E. J. Kane, *Economic Statistics and Econometrics* (New York: Harper & Row, 1968).
J. Kmenta, *Elements of Econometrics* (New York: Macmillan, 1971).
M. J. C. Surrey, *An Introduction to Econometrics* (Oxford: OUP, 1974).
A. A. Walters, *An Introduction to Econometrics*, 2nd edn (London: Macmillan, 1970).

ECONOMIC THEORY
R. G. Lipsey, *An Introduction to Positive Economics*, 4th edn (London: Weidenfeld & Nicolson, 1975).
P. A. Samuelson, *Economics*, 10th edn (New York: McGraw-Hill, 1976).

MATHEMATICS AND STATISTICS
G. C. Archibald and R. G. Lipsey, *An Introduction to a Mathematical Treatment of Economics*, 2nd edn (London: Weidenfeld & Nicolson, 1973).
H. T. Hayslett and P. Murphy, *Statistics Made Simple*, Made Simple series (London: W. H. Allen, 1968).
R. Morley, *Mathematics for Modern Economics* (London: Fontana, 1972).
M. R. Spiegel, *Theory and Problems of Statistics*, Schaum's Outline series (New York: McGraw-Hill, 1972).
K. A. Yeomans, *Statistics for the Social Scientist*, vols 1 and 2 (Harmondsworth: Penguin, 1968).

APPLIED ECONOMETRICS
M. Desai, *Applied Econometrics* (London: Philip Allan, 1976).
M. K. Evans, *Macroeconomic Activity* (New York: Harper & Row, 1969).
L. Wagner and N. Baltazzis, *Readings in Applied Microeconomics* (Oxford: The Clarendon Press/Open University, 1973).
R. Wynn and K. Holden, *Introduction to Applied Econometric Analysis* (London: Macmillan, 1974).

Index